A Two-Tiered Existence

SAMANTHA KANE

A TWO-TIERED EXISTENCE

Edited by
Sarah Harding

Published in 1998 by

Writers and Artists PLC
788-790 Finchley Road
London NW11 7UR

A catalogue record for this book is available from the British Library.

ISBN 0-9533604-0-7

Typeset by Writers and Artists PLC.

Printed and bound in Great Britain by
Cox & Wyman Ltd, Reading, Berkshire

This book is dedicated to my children, and all those who I loved and lost along the way. And to Sarah for her continuous support.

My first birthday, with my mother and father in the little villa in Zofaranaya.

Contents

Acknowledgement

My grateful thanks to Sarah Harding, who has done more than simply edit this book; and who is in no way to blame for any errors of a factual nature – or opinions, which are of course my own.

With my brother and sister, on a school trip in Baghdad.

A trip to Cairo with my family, 1975.

Childhood in Baghdad

Our narrative begins among the warm climes of the Middle East, where limitless deep-blue skies meet with the vaporous heat that rises from the scorching earth. If you travel approximately eight miles south of Baghdad, you come to the small suburb of Zofaranaya. During the summer months all sorts of exotic fruit – water melons, grapes, figs – are to be found ripening in the fields and vineyards of the neighbouring farms; and, further off, the low hum of combine harvesters provides a monotonous accompaniment to the chirping of the crickets. Within the suburb itself, small villas find shade from the continuous assault of the sun beneath neatly arranged groups of palm trees.

Zofaranaya is the place of my birth. It was in one of these villas that I lived with my parents for the first 17 years of my life, until the time when I finally left home. I was not an only child: apart from myself, my mother gave birth to two offspring – a boy and a girl. Together with the 16 cats that resided successively with us, we lived a life that ranged from moments of unhappiness to the most idyllic existence one can imagine. The earliest memories I have of this period stem from when I was about four years of age. These are memories of a little boy racing about the yard, with my brother in hot pursuit shooting at me with a make-believe gun. We would often disagree about who was going to be the cop and who should be the robber, and ended up fighting one another. My parents would look on with mild disapproval – until the moment when the scuffle began to get out of hand.

I always enjoyed the rough and tumble of boys' games – but although I was often to be found up to some mischief or other with my brother, in secret I harboured a kind of admiration for my sister. When she played with her dolls or rearranged the furniture in her tiny doll's house, I would glance at her with envy – there was something intriguing in the delicacy with which she arranged every aspect of her existence. Her bedroom seemed like a forbidden palace, containing delights hidden from the everyday sight of mortals! Yet, for all this, I did possess some idea of what goodies might be found in my sister's room.

I had ventured into my mother's bedroom on numerous occasions: arranged on a little oak dressing-table in the corner of the room I would find lipsticks, mascara, face powder, and a vast array of other products whose nature was a complete mystery to me. Sneaking a look in her wardrobe, I examined the innumerable brightly coloured blouses and dresses that I had frequently seen my mother wearing. Would I find the same items in my sister's bedroom?

When I was a little older, I was often alone in the house. On such occasions a wave of excitement would come over me; left on my own, I imagined that I could do anything I wanted – and with utter impunity! I was about six or seven years old at the time, and my fascination with the unexplored domain of my sister's room was more alive than ever. The opportunity was available: it was now or never! I eased the door gently, and it swung back noiselessly upon its hinges. I was confronted with an Aladdin's Cave! Dresses, dolls… scattered everywhere was the paraphernalia of little girls. I would have discarded my entire repertoire of guns and toy cars for just one of my sister's dolls!

It never occurred to me to question the nature of the interest that this room and its contents provoked: it simply possessed a mesmerising power over me. Perhaps it was just sheer curiosity. Whatever it was that attracted me, I was soon undressed and replacing my boys' clothes with those of my sister. It was strange, but a feeling of well-being seemed to pervade my soul as I exchanged my clothes.

I continued this practice for a number of years, always grasping the opportunity whenever it offered itself. Not long after that first occasion when I dressed up in my sister's clothes, I extended my activities to my mother's wardrobe and the dressing-table scattered with make-up. Eventually, I found that any period of abstention from these practices would result in a nervous pain in my stomach – and only when the house was empty was I able to find relief from this pain.

But this panacea for all my troubles was soon brought to an abrupt halt, when sporting what appeared to be my sister's party dress, with flounces terminating in a filigree of lace, I heard steps just outside the doorway of her bedroom. I froze on the spot, unable to make the least attempt to hide myself in the wardrobe or dart under the bed. The one or two seconds during which I awaited detection seemed an eternity. For a second time the door of the room swung back on its hinges, and in stepped my brother. The expression on his face was a mixture of severity and barely suppressed laughter. Involuntarily staring at my bright-red painted lips, he proceeded to chastise me. This was absolutely shameful, I was an embarrassment to himself and our father. Brought almost to tears by his harsh tone, I tried desperately to defend myself, advancing the most ridiculous excuses. But it was all the same to him – it simply would not do to parade round the house dressed up like a little girl! I hung my head in shame.

Perhaps pitying what he perceived to be a pathetic and embarrassing sight, he finally resolved not to tell anyone – with a single proviso, that I would put an immediate end to such behaviour. Never again did I possess the courage to enter my sister's room.

As the years passed I became aware that there was something profoundly wrong with me – but what it was I could never fathom with any degree of exactitude. Years before, I had frequently asked my father whether there existed any possibility that I might have been a girl – or, if that was not the case, whether I might perhaps grow into a girl as I got older. I would eagerly await some sign of affirmation in his voice, longing for him to say yes to my queries. But, of course, this never happened! Taking a firm hand, he would direct me to the final court of appeal – to my genitals, assuring me that my future would be determined by the tiny apparatus that dangled between my legs. How utterly terrible, I would muse, that such an insignificant item was capable of deciding how I was going to live my future! Both my mother and my father believed that it would only be a matter of time before I "grew out of it" and invested all their energy in encouraging me to join in with the boys more and to play a bit more football, if I could.

However, not all of the boys allowed me to join in their games; for some inexplicable reason they made rude gestures in my presence, referring to me as a "little girl". And there was a further reason that deterred me from my efforts to integrate with them. When I saw the other boys swimming or playing games together, I was conscious of slight anomalies between their bodies and mine. In addition to minor protuberances in my chest and the more extensive development of my nipples, I noticed that my body appeared altogether less hirsute than those of other boys. I felt deeply offended by their comments, and decided to avoid them whenever possible.

Events took a change for the better when I started secondary school, which was located about a mile from where I lived. It stood on the periphery of the suburb of Zofaranaya, a brightly painted two-storey building abutting onto an endless expanse of tomato plantations and grape vines, interspersed here and there with solitary copses. My parents possessed high hopes that within this institution my latent talents would at last begin to blossom, especially now I had overcome (so they thought) my "strange tendencies". Very quickly I made a number of new friends, and even found great enjoyment spending the hours after school playing football with them. With all my heart I can assert that I really did do all I could to suppress those particular manifestations of my character that my parents found so disturbing.

But like tends to seek like; and I found myself exposed to other boys of a feminine nature, who were extremely eager to befriend me. I say that I was "like" these individuals, but the only point of contact between myself and them was a symmetry that existed in our external behaviour. If two such opposed causes as transsexualism and homosexuality can result – at least at a single point – in identical effects, I was aware, at least, of the knowledge that I did not reside in the latter camp.

Taking time out with my brother and friends by Lake Habaniya, near Baghdad.

Divining a certain effeminacy in my behaviour, such individuals would seek me out and query the nature of my sexuality. This was difficult. While the boys about me were seeking girls in order to develop their sexual prowess, I remained totally inert, not knowing to which sex I felt primarily inclined. Girls were out of the question: they made me feel like a man. In my desire to experience womanhood only one option was left open to me: boys. Thus in response to their queries I would depict myself as a practitioner of sodomy.

The grounds adjoining the school provided ideal cover for the secret activities that followed – or if I felt daring, I would take one of my friends home when my parents and brother and sister were absent. In each case – whether among the tomatoes or in my bedroom – I insisted on playing the passive role. Only then was I able to achieve a feeling of womanhood. Sometimes I even went so far as to make myself up for these encounters, to intensify the desired effect.

With maybe one exception, I never found any of the boys I had sexual relations with particularly attractive. What interested me primarily was the thrill of adopting a passive role, imagining myself as a pretty woman being ravished. Strangely, my academic performance was greatly enhanced by these activities – as if the satisfaction of my desire to feel like a woman enabled me to channel my energy into more productive areas than before.

Just as one week gives birth to its identical brother, so did the cycle of my life return to a scene already described. Seizing an opportunity while the house was empty, I decided to entertain one of my friends in my accustomed manner. Lying prostrate on the bed, I was in the act of offering myself in what I believed to be the manner of a woman when my brother once again entered the room. I will pass over the torrent of abuse he directed at me – my companion pulling up his trousers, tripping up, and dashing from the house – and the tears and shame that followed. There was simply nothing I could do.

My position was hopeless. It was only those prohibited activities that had yielded me some degree of solace.

Yet I could neither continue them, for fear of their being disclosed to my parents, nor suppress the feeling inside me that demanded recognition. I was 15 years of age – another year hence and I would be able to leave my family and do whatever I felt necessary in order achieve some measure of equanimity.

My only avenue of escape was to adopt a course of action that would satisfy those around me. I judged it might be opportune to start growing some facial hair. Although at that time my face was still soft and hairless (showing only the first signs of "bum fluff"), I aped other boys of my age and shaved the soft down from my face. This would have to do for now, I mused.

Ultimately, as soon as I was old enough to go my own way, the frustration, the despondency and the sadness that all too often transformed itself into violence left me with no option but to leave Baghdad. Even though I would miss everyone sorely.

My parents were upset when I informed them that I would be leaving. For interminable hours they assailed me with a barrage of remonstrances, querying my reason for what they believed to be a sudden decision to leave. It did not help my case when I broke the news to them that I was going to travel to England to study engineering. My mother pointed out that there were good colleges in Baghdad; that I would be compelled to learn a new language, eat foreign food, and adopt a new culture. All this was a small price to pay for my freedom. Soon, however, my parents became resigned to my decision, and the time came to leave Baghdad.

*

Gathered around the goalposts that had often witnessed the cries of happiness that can only issue from those blithely unaware of the future, 10 or 12 young men stood laughing and taunting one another good-naturedly. Together on this playing field they had often spent valuable hours playing football, with their schoolwork stowed safely in their satchels. Suddenly a solemn air pervaded their expressions. A pledge was being pronounced: "On this day in 1977 we all pledge that on the selfsame day in the year 2000 we shall once again gather at this spot beside the goalposts and each shall relate the course of his life from this moment to that." Hands were clasped, fraternal embraces exchanged, and each member of that jovial group went off intent on fulfilling the aim of living a life to surpass all dreams.

I said farewell to all my friends and neighbours, knowing that I would never again see them as they were then, nor ever again set eyes on my home as it was. How frightening life is! Kissing each of the 16 cats that had befriended me throughout the years of my growth from boyhood to manhood, I departed – leaving my entire world behind.

With my suitcases packed in the boot of my father's car, we drove together in silence through modern Baghdad and then on to the Old City, parts of which have survived for 1500 years. Finally, after crossing the bridge that divides the Old City, we followed the meandering River Tigris, until our journey terminated at Baghdad International Airport.

Peering through the misty window beside me, beyond the wing of the aeroplane bound for England I could make out the city of Baghdad. The bustling and noise had all now died way; and all that remained in my vision looked like a child's plaything, a tiny town with buildings constructed in miniature.

Within that tiny city infinite hopes, misery and joy had found expression – *my* hopes, *my* joy, *my* misery. How dear it was to me! As the plane slowly ascended above the silk-like clouds, Baghdad bid its final goodbye to me. Lost in the world of my dreams, the city of my childhood would for ever remain departed from me.

With the pigeons in Trafalgar Square, during my first year in Britain.

My Early Life in Britain

With all the excitement of a child, I arrived in London possessing a minimum of both language and money. I was an alien in more than one way! But I did not mind in the least. I had entered an entirely new world, where my demand for freedom seemed to dissolve with the problems that had initially given rise to it. I was liberated!

Nevertheless, not everything was as straightforward as I had anticipated – and for the first time in my life I was confronted with the hardships involved in being completely self-sufficient. Residing in Brighton, in what can only be described as a hovel, I spent the first six months of my time in England studying at an English-language school.

Ever since I had said goodbye to my parents I had experienced the most profound sense of compunction, coupled with the urge to live according to their wishes, both in suppressing the need I often felt to adopt female practices and in enrolling on an engineering course. Accordingly, as soon as I had acquired a more-or-less tolerable grasp of the English language, I departed for Swindon and studied for a National Diploma in engineering, in preparation for entering university in London.

So far everything had happened at lightning speed, allowing me little opportunity to ponder on the problems that I had encountered earlier in my life. But once I became a regular student the pace began to slacken off and the novelty of my residence in England to some extent dissipated. Regarding the English as a nation that lived on fish-and-chips and roast beef and Yorkshire pudding (and, between them, an unhappy mixture of the overpowering and the insipid!), I was dismayed every time I sat down to eat. My imperfect grasp of the language frustrated me greatly. And on top of this I had to deal with poverty.

The re-entrance into my life of my earlier dilemmas could therefore not have come at a more inopportune moment. Whenever I happened to set my eyes upon women, I experienced an ineffable desire to become as they were. If at that time I had been aware of the option of undergoing a sex change, I am sure I would have ignored the promise that I had made to my parents and forged straight ahead with transforming myself. But, of course, I had no idea that gender reassignment was even a possibility!

The old pains in my stomach soon returned. With the sheer weight of pressure that I was undergoing I found myself frequently visiting the doctor with tales of blackouts and severe pains. I felt as though I was going to die. All I could do to keep my head above water was to concentrate on my problems one by one – beginning with the urgent need to resolve my financial difficulties.

The days were taken up with my engineering studies, so in order to consolidate my economic independence I set about launching a business of my own that I could operate during the evenings. Having obtained the necessary licences, I converted a Volkswagen camper into a mobile kitchen, making use of the college workshop facilities to install my modifications. In this vehicle I could be seen late at night serving hot dogs and hamburgers to an unwieldy, and frequently aggressive, crowd.

On a cool summer night in 1979, finding that my vending activities had been prematurely curtailed by the rapid consumption of hot dogs and hamburgers, I closed up my camper and prepared myself for a night of dancing. After donning a three-piece suit that would find its only rival in John Travolta's, I set off with a premonition that this night would change my life.

As I entered the Brunell Disco I was deafened by the tumultuous ebb of the music, and a vast wave of raised voices, laughter and raillery submerged me within its intoxicating atmosphere. The darkness, and the frequently dazzling lights, limited my vision so I could only see what was immediately in front of me. My senses had retracted to a point.

Ordering myself a meagre half-pint of lager and a packet of nuts, I aimlessly attempted to make myself comfortable on a blue-leatherette bar stool. It was impossible! Like a mass of cattle frenziedly forcing their way into an inadequately-sized pen, vast hordes of people disturbed both my drink and my repose as they crashed blindly into my stool. Much more of this and I would be leaving!

Between the flashing of the lights and my continual fidgeting upon the stool, I saw a girl whose appearance affected me profoundly. I had never encountered such an experience before. Up to that moment I had been completely indifferent to girls; this was something new and unaccustomed. I felt as if my eyes had met with a radiating nucleus of beauty. It was as if every atom of my being had been pierced with alpha rays. Before this wingless seraph, this pure form of beauty, I could do nothing but offer my complete submission. It was her *form* that enraptured me – the utter perfection of her features, the undulating curves of her hips and breasts.

How I wanted to bathe in the glory of this being! To unify my existence with hers; to submerge myself in her; to lose my individuality, my body, in her. I sought blindly to understand the precise intent of my desire. I was lost. I desired everything of her, I desired *annihilation.* Only so could I unify my being with her perfection; in her I would find peace. I asked her for a dance.

Within an instant my hopes were dashed. This bright paradise, placed alluringly within the wilderness of life, had retreated, casting me once again into the open, boundless steppes. A single utterance, fixed into the fortifications of *custom*, had destroyed my chance of attaining perfection. I could do nothing. Why I felt so shaken by her refusal I did not know. Without thought, I bounded headlong into the crowded darkness, every segment of my being lost in complete disorientation. Gyrating in all directions, not knowing where I was going, reeling and pushing, I lost myself in oblivion.

When I emerged from the darkness, I found that without any conscious effort of my own I had travelled full circle. Once again I stood before her. I remained motionless. Glancing sideways at her sister, she giggled, laughed, and whispered "It's him again!"

*

This divine creature whom I adored so passionately was to become my wife and the mother of our two children. My love for her would never undergo the slightest dissipation. Throughout all the appalling scenes that finally extinguished our life together, my love, as if existing beyond this physical world, always remained immutable.

My desire had set blinkers upon my vision. Like all true lovers, I never allowed a single word or action to contaminate the object of my love. I promised to provide her with a future of unsurpassable riches – notwithstanding the fact that I was a poor student selling hot dogs! Not surprisingly she did not believe me, and I did not possess a monopoly on her affections. But if she would merely permit me to be her chief sycophant – *that was enough.*

But soon the love I had received from her was cut short, when I left Swindon to continue my studies in London. This, I thought, would be the last time I ever saw her.

*

When I arrived in London I enrolled on a course in aeronautical engineering. Whether thoughts of my past love inhibited the success of my studies, or I was simply not made for constructing aeroplanes out of what appeared to be a pile of scrap metal, I decided to take a change in direction. For the next three years I studied for an HND in engineering, finally graduating in 1983. And then, once my studies were completed, I found myself at a loose end.

One evening I received a telephone call from a former friend, Tiqwan, in Swindon. He asked me if I would like to stay with him for a while. I readily accepted his invitation – for, other considerations apart, I had absolutely nothing else to do – and found myself back in Swindon the following day. That evening we dined together and reminisced over past events. Almost as if it was a matter of no interest to me, Tiqwan suddenly said "Do you remember that girl you went out with all those years ago?" He did not even need to mention her name. Mesmerised, I could only manage a nod of assent. "Well," he continued, "I spoke to her the other day and she asked me about you..."

Though it may perhaps sound strange, I had hoped that my former girlfriend would be married after all these years. In retrospect, I had not enjoyed the experience of falling in love. In fact, I had found it particularly unpleasant. Yet somehow I felt exulted that I might still find in her a desire to be with me; that I might care for her; that I might protect her beauty from the onslaught of the world.

The following day I found her at home. Seeing her, I knew that I would have done anything within my power to secure her as my beloved. I again offered to bestow upon her an abundant future. She accepted my offer with alacrity, and I was simply over the moon!

If at that moment anyone would have charged me with the accusation that perhaps I too was a woman, and that my marriage was hopelessly doomed because of this fact, I would have rebuked them out of hand and told them that was utter nonsense.

Determined only to fulfil the rash promises I had made, I sought every means to bring my plans to fruition. I sold all I owned; I contracted loans with every and any bank that would offer me credit; I worked until the very desire for sleep had departed from my body. And all of this I placed at the feet of my beloved. In the autumn of 1984, we were married in a quaint village church near Swindon. Only a single element was lacking to make our life together perfect. And, indeed, after nine months of our marriage my wife gave birth to the first little bundle of bliss and happiness that possessed us of the key to paradise.

The birth itself came as something of a shock to me. During the preceding months, along with my wife I had attended weekly prenatal classes, supposedly designed to encourage me to empathise with her during her period of labour. It had all been very straightforward. Lying down beside her, I would breath in and out in time with her simulated contractions, then after a designated period we would go home. Very easy, or so I thought.

But perhaps I had become too accustomed to this easy routine. When the time actually came – 9 o'clock on the night of May 27th, 1985 – my wife called down to me from the bedroom "Sam, my contractions are beginning." I dashed upstairs. Lying down beside her, I proceeded to perform my breathing exercises. "No," she cried in desperation, "I need to go to the hospital!" Jumping up from the bed, I ran downstairs, started our broken-down old Citroën, stowed my wife safely in the passenger seat, and we were off.

By now her contractions were becoming more and more frequent. We simply had to get to the hospital as quickly as possible. As I navigated the bends in the road like a racing driver, a wave of desperation came over me. Were my wife's attempts to distract me from my overwhelming anxiety an indication that I was too late? That she was about to give birth here, in this broken-down Citroën? Then she gestured to the right, and my anxiety immediately dissipated. Pointing in the direction of a Chinese takeaway, she demanded that I stop the car and dash in to get her a portion of spare-ribs and chips.

Without pausing to question the wisdom of her request, I darted from the car and burst into the take-away. "I need service quickly," I explained to the fellow taking orders. "My wife's about to have a baby, and it's imperative she gets some spare-ribs and chips!" But he was preoccupied with ascertaining the validity of a suspicious £20 note that the customer before me was trying to pass off in payment for his food, and my desperation went more or less unnoticed. What could I do? Grabbing the note from the still pondering assistant, I snatched equivalent notes from my wallet and thrust them at him in exchange for the suspect item. Finally, I obtained my order!

We arrived at the hospital in good time; and our first baby, a girl, was not born until noon the following day. After pacing up and down the corridors all night, but for the unquenchable joy I felt at the advent of this new life I am sure my legs would have given way beneath me! When at last the time arrived for the birth of our daughter, I felt I simply could not contain the elation that pervaded my soul. Never before had I experienced such unlimited happiness. When my wife handed the little bundle to me to hold – no heavier than a bag of sugar – I felt I was going to burst for joy!

As if my life was not perfect enough, on September 25th of the following year my wife gave birth to our second child – this time a boy. During the years that followed, the love I felt for our two children overshadowed all other aspects of my existence. Together, my wife and our children defined the limits of my reality; beyond our life together nothing but a barren desert of untold misery persisted. My wife, son and daughter – *in these three figures my existence was summed up.*

*

It may seem paradoxical that I found nothing questionable in the role I was adopting. Perhaps I supposed that the problems I had been experiencing regarding my gender identity would in some unexplained way simply vanish now I was married. But, on reflection, I am inclined to locate the truth of the situation in the fact that I simply found it very easy at that time of extreme happiness to ignore experiences the nature of which I had always been suspicious of. In fact, I deplored the nature of these experiences. I saw in them a threat to my masculinity, to my life; and I now regarded them as a rather weak and easily conquerable experience.

For all that, my relationship with my wife did sometimes smack of the idiosyncratic. To assert in retrospect that I believed she was aware, however vaguely, of the disturbances in my gender may seem like a case of rationalisation. Yet both the events of our relationship and the terms in which she often reproached me argue strongly in favour of its truth. For example, it would be incorrect to say that she thought of me as a husband. As a brother, a sister, or perhaps even a girlfriend – but never *simply as a man.* Lying together on the sofa, we would gossip together like two young girls – she telling me about the individuals she found attractive and I listening to her comments without the slightest jealousy. She was my ideal, and through her I lived my life.

But though I tried to the utmost of my ability to fulfil her every desire, she would often utter words of sorrow and lament the shattered years of her childhood. *I felt like a failure* – the mere fact that she appeared always to be reflecting on her past seemed indicative of an empty and lifeless present. My attempts to lift the burden that weighed so heavily upon her failed hopelessly. I believed I could assuage her suffering by adding glitter and tinsel to the exterior of our marriage. Egoistic in my attempts to alleviate her sorrow, I hoped my gifts might somehow plumb the bottomless well of her heart, that the misery of her existence could be relieved by material things. "How could someone so beautiful possess so much unhappiness?" Never did my sympathy and compassion delve any deeper.

Spurred by these thoughts, I intensified my efforts to provide my wife with a luxurious life. I launched two companies – one importing fruit and vegetables, the other manufacturing and selling computers. And I worked day and night to achieve the objectives I had set myself. Some years later, a chance opportunity led me to align my business activities with those of a wealthy Saudi Arabian sheikh. We launched a property and investment company, which eventually culminated, in 1990, in my notorious bid to take over Sheffield United football club – one of the most controversial takeovers in the history of football.

I have always wanted to play for Yorkshire, so I bought Headingley

At the press conference announcing my bid to take over Sheffield United football club.

Soccer Boss

It is often said that money "talks". Indeed, its voice penetrates to every corner of the world, overcoming all boundaries of class and ethnic distinctions.

Gazing out of the rain-drenched window of my Grosvenor Street office in Mayfair, the sudden ring of the telephone distracted me from the cold winter's day. It was a wealthy friend from Manchester. "Sam," he exclaimed excitedly, "you simply must catch the first available flight to Manchester. I've a wonderful investment opportunity for you to consider – in football. By the way, bring the company lawyer with you." His excitement was contagious. My curiosity propelled me to the airport immediately.

It was 1990. The chairman and majority shareholder of Manchester United, Martin Edwards, had made a contract with a business man, Michael Knighton, to discharge his shares in the club for £10,000,000. Knowing that I was managing funds for a rich Saudi sheikh, the proposal had been offered to my company to provide funding for the prospective buyer.

As a boy in Iraq, I had been a great fan of Manchester United – long before I even knew the whereabouts of England, let alone Manchester. I was infused with all the ardour of my childhood again. The possibility of investing in such a monumentally successful football team thrilled me. This was the business opportunity of a lifetime. The Old Trafford ground itself was worth far in excess of the majority shares – not to mention the collective value of the players!

One problem presented itself. Everything, the exchange of money included, had to be completed within 24 hours, when the contract between Martin Edwards and Michael Knighton was due to expire. Given a large team of smart lawyers and accountants, it would be difficult to arrange payment of such an enormous sum as £10,000,000 within *weeks*. How, then, could this be achieved in a single day? There was nothing for it: in the end the offer had to be declined, and I was back to the prosaic events of the previous days. Michael Knighton, however, became a director of Manchester United, and later chairman of third division Carlisle United.

*

But the past was to repeat itself once again. I was sitting at a table in Blond's – a restaurant I owned in

Dover Street, London – awaiting the arrival of Len Brealey. The arrangements had been made by Michael Knighton. Apparently he wanted to discuss a business deal with me. Sitting there, wondering what he had in mind, I noticed the entrance of a very tall well-built man, grey from head to toe – grey hair, grey suit. Len Brealey, chairman of the offshore trust that owned Sheffield United, had arrived.

Folded under his arm was a copy of *The Racing Times*. This was a man who was down to earth in the extreme. With the flippant manner of a market trader, he would conduct business deals worth millions of pounds as if he was selling a pound of tomatoes – straight to the matter in hand, no time wasted! He was sharp and very much to the point: Sheffield United was mine if I wished to purchase the shares in his possession.

Pending my decision, Reg Brealey, the chairman of Sheffield United and the brother of Len, invited me to be his guest at a football match the following Saturday. With his carefully studied manner, Reg introduced me to the board of directors. Unknown to me, one of the directors, Paul Woolhouse, was preparing to raise the necessary sum to purchase the club in opposition to my bid. He looked at me askance, with penetrating eyes.

During the days that followed the directors displayed an increasing sense of uneasiness – with the more conservative members of the board showing signs of contention. Everything therefore had to be done right away, otherwise the whole deal would be off. The contracts were signed by the end of the week. The deal, based on shared options, had been concluded.

Sport

SPURS HAVE BETRAYED MANAGER TERRY VENABLES SAYS JOHN GILES—SEE PAGE 38

Harry cashes in

Bassett welcomes £5m Arab takeover

By JIMMY ARMFIELD

DAVE BASSETT last night drove Sheffield United a step nearer Wembley and then welcomed the Arab takeover, which could fully restore the club's former glory.

Bassett, who collects exotic bosses, watched his team beat Barnsley 1-0 in their FA Cup fifth round second replay before talking about the latest millionaire to walk into his life.

FA CUP CRACKER

Agana spot on at last

TONY AGANA'S penalty ... seconds into extra-time last night landed the Blades a jackpot quarter-final against Manchester United on Sunday.

On March 1st, a profusion of photographers and reporters fought their way into Sheffield United's administrative buildings. All were agog with the expectation of catching the important news that Sheffield United had been taken over by a new man. But who? A press conference of unparalleled proportions was held. An announcement was made: Sam Hashimi, investing capital of Arab origin, had become the new chairman of Sheffield United football club. By the close of that day, the news had become an international issue.

All at once Paul Woolhouse emerged on the scene, offering a counter bid in an effort to oppose my take-over. He found a ready ally in David Bassett, the manager of the club, whose earlier adherence to my bid appeared to be very far from steadfast. During a BBC documentary entitled *United,* Paul Woolhouse claimed that a number of the board members – including David Bassett – were unhappy about the possibility of my take-over materialising. If this happened, he asserted, there was a growing possibility that these individuals might leave the club, together with a number of the players. This would jeopardise the imminent success of the club.

The contention continued without end, one side gaining the upper hand, followed by the other. Supporter was pitched against supporter, and the whole thing was just waiting to split wide open. "We don't want this Iraqi invading our club!", shouted one side. "He's the best thing that's happened to Sheffield United in ages!", retorted the other. The media was fascinated by the whole messy affair, and closely watched and reported every twist and turn.

Whatever my opponents might have said of me, the plans I formed with regard to the future of Sheffield United were made with the best interests of the club in mind. To bring increased revenue to the club, I had completed plans with my Middle East consortium to develop the adjoining land into a hotel, shopping complex and multi-screen cinema. Everything was ready, the capital was in place. A further effect of these developments would be the introduction of families to football. Both the stadium and the planned complex would incorporate facilities designed to make a family day out at the football ground a viable option.

I had envisaged a club of international proportions. To make Sheffield United into one of the greatest teams in England I was to promote it worldwide, launching it from its regional existence into supranational dimensions. The capital generated from all these activities, from which ever corner of the globe it was derived, would have ended up in Sheffield, building a glorious and prosperous future for a great British team.

But the extreme Left were against me all the way. The whole question of football financing was at stake. Somewhat reactionary in their conception of football management the Left – together with Richard Caborn, the MP for Sheffield Central acting as their vanguard – argued that the plans I had put together would be the utter ruin of the club. The issue was then taken to the House of Commons, with Mr Caborn urging the Sports Minister to intervene in my takeover.

Soon the Saudi Arabian consortium began to display signs of uneasiness. I was now under attack from all sides and experiencing increasing difficulty in attracting supporters for my bid. The King of Saudi Arabia himself was reported to have found it necessary to express his disapproval!

But even if I could have succeeded in reversing the tide of opinion that was threatening to sweep away all my efforts, I could never have anticipated nor hoped to rebut what was about to descend upon me through the hand of destiny. With the news that a Sheffield company had been supplying Iraq with the materials necessary for the construction of a "supergun" and, compounded with this, the Iraqi invasion of Kuwait, my final death throes were initiated once and for all. The game was up. My bid was dead in its tracks.

Nevertheless, I retained my unremitting interest in the football industry and continued to try to convince my investors to approve the financing of my plans. At this time I was also approached by Terry Venables, the former England coach, who sought my funding to purchase Tottenham Hotspur, which he was currently managing. However, I had experienced some of the problems that can arise when nationalities come into conflict – and it seemed extremely risky to consider using finance of Arab origin to fund a club with strong Jewish connections. Accordingly, Terry Venables found an alternative partner in Alan Sugar.

When finally my labours – though not my heart – had departed from Sheffield United, Paul Woolhouse procured the chairmanship that I so dearly desired.

The year following the demise of my efforts to take over Sheffield United I received a telephone call from a metal company based in Belgium. Paul Woolhouse, they claimed, owed their company a substantial amount of money, and it would be of help to them if I could fly to Belgium and provide them with any information I possessed regarding him.

As I looked out of the window of the aeroplane, a feeling of immense satisfaction pervaded my being. I sincerely hoped that the file resting on my lap would secure Paul Woolhouse's downfall. But following his resignation from Sheffield United in 1992, he vanished from the scene. It was said that he had departed to the sunny climes of Australia. The origin of the capital with which he obtained the chairmanship of Sheffield United was finally revealed to all.

Paul Woolhouse's departure was followed by the good news that Reg Brealey had once again taken over the chairmanship of Sheffield United. In the role of Middle East representative, I invited the club to travel to the UAE making use of my favourable connection with the son of the ruler of the United Arab Emirates, Sheikh Abdula bin Zayid Al-Nahyan, chairman of the Olympic Committee.

*

The aeroplane landed at Dubai airport. Donning Arab national costume – a white robe and head shawls – I awaited the Sheffield team, alongside important club officials from Abu Dhabi. At once, as if from a megaphone, the words "Sam, Sam? Is that Sam?"

bellowed from the exit of the aeroplane. They had arrived. I was bombarded with a barrage of questions, as they shoved past one another to gain access to me. "Where is our hotel?" "Are there going to be many camels about?" And so on and so forth. They expected to see something akin to the "Lost City", a complex that had stood outside the flow of time – and some disappointment could be detected when they found themselves in "just another city".

Thus in 1993 David Bassett had the good fortune to prepare his team's international players for the 1994 World Cup beneath the limitless azure skies of Arabia – instead of on the rain-drenched fields of Sheffield. Never before had Sheffield United experienced such a boon! Yet, despite David Bassett's determination to motivate the team, it is true to say that it was a holiday atmosphere, rather than one of work, that animated the team that week. And though the local media found no grounds to approve of Sheffield United's performance, a great time was enjoyed by all! A pleasant swan song, indeed, both to my marriage and to my activities in the football industry.

IT'S

Sam: 'I'm no Arabian Knighton'

By JOHN EDWARDS

TAKEOVER tycoon Sam Hashimi last night provided the assurance all football wanted to hear.

After coughing up a cool £5m for control of Sheffield United and promising manager Dave Bassett millions for new players, the 32-year-old whizz-kid pledged: "I'm not another Michael Knighton."

Hashimi wanted to step in as buyer when the Knighton shambles left Manchester United's world-famous empire under the auctioneer's hammer with a £30m reserve price on it.

Now he wants to mould the Blades into another United — with one reservation.

"The Knighton affair was a fiasco, and there's no chance of that being repeated here," he insisted.

"The agreement I have struck with Sheffield United is watertight, and I can assure everyone that there will be no embarrassments in this takeover.

"I have given assurances to the board on that score."

Prince

The Iraqi-born businessman was installed as vice-chairman, and will replace Reg Brealey as chairman at the end of the season.

The club's new owner drew on his own personal fortune to finance the deal, but admitted he also had the backing of money from the Middle East.

Hashimi — already referred to as Mr Sam within Bramall Lane — was coy about their exact identity.

But they are known to include four sheiks and a prince, with the major figure being the Mayor of Jeddah, Sheik Abdul Momenah.

The consortium's Mr Big also owns Jeddah FC

DEAL: Brealey (left) and Hashimi yesterday

— who play amid the splendour of a sumptuous £50m stadium — and is the head of a huge property empire.

Hashimi, who has built up multi-business interests since arriving in England as a student 15 years ago, is the front man, though.

And his opening address will have been music to manager Bassett's ears.

Ambition

"I believe totally in our manager's ability, and if he thinks he needs new players then money will be made available," he said.

"We will compete for million-pound players if that's what Dave thinks is needed to make sure this club gets into the First Division.

"My ambition is for Sheffield United to compete with the likes of Liverpool, Manchester United and Arsenal."

The deal was threatened by a boardroom revolt when furious directors called an emergency meeting to thrash out details and ask Brealey for the chance to match Hashimi's offer.

Brealey revealed: "I allayed certain fears during a frank and open discussion, and I'm glad to say the board have stayed intact and given their blessing to the takeover."

Paul Woolhouse, whose 12.5 per cent stake makes him the second biggest shareholder, said:

"One point we wanted to be sure of was that shares would come back to the board if Mr Hashimi withdrew from the club."

Hashimi added: "Football has been a very important part of my life ever since I was a small boy.

"No-one in the Middle-East realised that football clubs over here could be for sale until news emerged of events at Manchester United last year."

Hashimi and his backers will begin talks shortly on ringing the ground with a hotel, cinema, sports club, shops and restaurant.

Man Utd director accepts explanation

HASHIMI SETTLES KNIGHTON CUP ROW

SAM HASHIMI: no sarcasm

By Tony Pritchett

SAM Hashimi, Sheffield United's new owner-in-waiting, has smoothed relationships with Michael Knighton of Manchester United before the teams meet in the quarter-final of the FA Cup on Sunday.

MICHAEL KNIGHTON: not amused

The Old Trafford director was upset at comments following Mr Hashimi's arrival at Bramall Lane this week and press headlines quoting Hashimi as saying he was "no Arabian Knighton."

It followed Hashimi's comments that he would like to meet the crowd in a formal manner on Sunday and a joking inquiry if he would run out with the team —as Knighton did before his takeover deal collapsed in embarrassment and acrimony.

The new Lane chief said today: "Michael Knighton saw the headlines and was not amused. But I have spoken with him and he understands I meant no sarcasm at his expense.

"We are good friends: I knew him before I became involved in Sheffield and am looking forward to seeing him before the Cup tie."

Successful

Hashimi and outgoing chairman Reg Brealey — the man from whom the controlling share interest is being bought — were due to meet again this afternoon, probably to settle final details of the sale although the deal is already said to be "watertight."

I understand that Brealey could miss the Manchester United match. He has provisional arrangements to fly back to India on Friday for important meetings concerning his Titaghur Jute company in Calcutta.

Hashimi hopes to complete his London business in time to travel to Sheffield on Friday and take an opportunity to introduce himself to the players.

He said: "I am delighted that we have such a big Cup tie in the stadium against such famous opponents. I will have nothing special to say to the players but I would like them to see my face and recognise me.

"But my main aim on Sunday is to meet the supporters.

Sheffield United taken over in £5m Middle East deal

By Colin Wright and William Johnson

SHEFFIELD United were yesterday taken over by a Middle East consortium fronted by Sam Hashimi, an Iraqi-born businessman, in a deal believed to be worth around £5 million.

Mr Hashimi, 32, a London-based financier, bought 51 per cent of the club's shares from Reg Brealey, the chairman, who had been looking to reduce his 63 per cent stake, built up when he underwrote an unsuccessful share issue nine years ago.

The purchase, the final price of which has not been confirmed, has been arranged through the Anglo-Arab Investment Company of which Mr Hashimi is managing director.

It was settled yesterday after an emergency meeting of the Sheffield United board at which Mr Brealey assured his five fellow directors that it was in the best interests of the club, currently second in Division Two.

Mr Hashimi said: "The finance for this deal has come partly from myself and partly from investment capital in the Middle East. I can understand supporters being concerned, but they need not worry. We have the best interests of the club at heart.

"I want to see Sheffield United become one of the great clubs of European football and negotiations will shortly begin to make Bramall Lane one of the most modern stadiums in Europe."

The new owner said that he and his financial backers had been looking for a year for the "right" English soccer club in which to invest. He added that substantial amounts of money would be made available to buy players, not just improve facilities, to help win promotion to the First Division.

Mr Hashimi said he wanted to foster links with the Middle East and added: "I admit I am connected with the Mayor of Jeddah [Sheik Abdul Momenah]."

News of the deal leaked at the weekend and prompted Sheffield directors to call yesterday's meeting. Mr Brealey, whose stake in the club has been reduced from 63 per cent to 11 per cent, did not give his fellow directors first option to buy him out.

But they agreed with the sale of his shares subject to an undertaking from Mr Hashimi and his backers that they would be offered first option should the consortium pull out. Sheffield United are £3m in debt, mainly to members of the board, who were told at the extraordinary meeting that the consortium would reduce the figure to £500,000.

Mr Brealey, 52, said he would continue as chairman "for the time being", with Mr Hashimi acting as vice-chairman. He insisted that the jobs of Dave Bassett, the manager, and Derek Dooley, the managing director, would not be affected by the sale.

"We have got to be ahead of the situation and this money has put us a division ahead," said Mr Brealey. "We can't go on expecting our manager, Dave Bassett, to find a player at £35,000 and turn him into a £1 million player.

"This is the best thing to happen to the club in 10 years. During the last two years I have discussed my shareholding with many interested parties but only Sam Hashimi showed a passionate interest in the game and the future of the club."

New move to block Lane takeover

LET ME BUY UNITED

Paul Woolhouse . . . unconditional

By Tony Pritchett

SHEFFIELD United director Paul Woolhouse this afternoon began a move to block the takeover of the club by Iraqi-born Sam Hashimi and his Middle East backers.

Woolhouse has tabled an unconditional offer to buy out chairman Reg Brealey in a deal which could cost him over £6 million.

Woolhouse bid could cost £6m

Hashimi, introduced at the club on Monday as the new owner of United, was said to have "a watertight agreement" to buy 51 percent of the club, leaving Brealey with 12 percent.

But Woolhouse, who led the Board in expressing concern at the Hashimi deal, said that since Monday he had been invited to make an offer for the shares.

Said Woolhouse: "That shows how watertight the agreement was. I have made an offer for all Mr Brealey's shares and it does not depend on any outline planning permission at the stadium. And the deal can be completed in a matter of weeks."

Informed of the Woolhouse offer this afternoon Brealey, on business in India, said: "We left all doors open at the last board meeting. There was an agreement that the directors would have an opportunity to make a counter bid."

Despite this Brealey had announced on Monday that the Board had "given their blessing to the arrangements I have made subject to one or two protective measures"

Introduced

Hashimi was introduced as the new owner — but Brealey insisted that the price for the deal had not been finalised; a strange situation which was not explained.

Sam Hashimi

Before the Woolhouse offer was made public there had been a clash between Mr Hashimi and the director about his plan to appear before the fans at tomorrow's Cup quarter final against Manchester United.

Hashimi had planned a tour of the ground and a talk to the players but the Lane directors, led by Woolhouse, the majority shareholder in the city in the absence of Brealey, had asked him to stay away.

When Hashimi indicated that it was still his plan to appear at the match, Mr Woolhouse said: "If he arrives at the ground, he will be turned away." Another director, Michael Wragg, said: "There is no way we can contemplate having Mr Hashimi in our directors' box on Sunday."

The Board, in the absence of Brealey and Alan Laver who is also abroad, insisted that Hashimi stay away "until his personal and financial credentials have been established beyond doubt."

Hashimi had replied to claims about his education and business background posed by the other directors and had challenged Mr Woolhouse to prove his commitment to the club.

Woolhouse, a director for three years, the second largest shareholder and a generous benefactor behind the scenes, has always shunned the limelight and did not wish his financial generosity to be made public.

But at the end of a crisis week at the club he raised the funds to make the counter offer.

If Woolhouse's offer is accepted — as I believe it will be — Mr Brealey will be left without any shares and will leave the club he has bossed for ten years.

Hashimi's plan would have seen Brealey continue, first as chairman and then as vice-chairman. And it would almost certainly have led to a move for Woolhouse to resign.

This could have sparked resignations from other directors.

Managing director Derek Dooley commented: "This whole affair is so unfortunate. We are on the eve of our biggest match in 22 years but find ourselves embroiled in politics.

"I would have preferred Hashimi to stay in the background until tomorrow's match is over and then come to Sheffield for a private disc..."

SAM'S FAMILY

Loved ones in Baghdad blitz

FLAMBOYANT Iraqi businessman Sam Hashimi, the one-time "owner" of Sheffield United, has revealed his family are caught up in the blitz of Baghdad.

Mr Hashimi's father, mother, sister and brother live in the Iraqi capital which is being devastated by pinpoint bombing from allied forces.

He has been unable to contact his father, a retired teacher, and can only hope his family are safe as destruction rains down from the sky.

"They are in the middle of this bombing — I'm very concerned about them as there is no communication with them," he said.

By Mike O'Sullivan

Sam Hashimi . . . fears for family's safety

"In Baghdad, all the military installations are in the middle of residential areas. I don't know why it's built like that, but there would be some element of damage in these areas from the bombing.

"There's been enough bombing. It should be

get him to pull his forces out of Kuwait. I don't want to see British soldiers killed or anybody else for that matter."

Resentment

London-based Mr Hashimi was probably the most famous Iraqi in

Hussein's invasion of Kuwait on August 2.

Mr Hashimi worked out a £6.25 million deal to buy Sheffield United from former Blades chairman Reg Brealey last March and was paraded as the new "owner" at Bramall Lane.

board, and Mr Brealey eventually sold the club to fellow director Paul Woolhouse.

The Gulf War may also have destroyed Mr Hashimi's lingering hopes of building up a Middle East marketing operation for the Blades.

Now, Mr Hashimi, who has an English wife and British citizenship, is feeling the backlash of public resentment.

"It's very difficult — there are some people saying it's a problem with Saddam Hussein and others think its a quarrel between the Iraqi people and the British."

He is having to deal with questions from his two children, aged five and six, over the safety of their grandparents and other relations.

And an Iraqi member of staff at his restaurant near

A Descent

The entire infrastructure of my business activities had been violently shaken. The "supergun" issue, together with the Iraqi invasion of Kuwait, provided my opponents within football with the means to quash my attempted take-over bid for Sheffield United once and for all. The upshot of this was that Sheikh Momin – the source of my business capital – became doubtful of my ability to manage his funds efficiently. Seizing the opportunity to create a radical breach between myself and the sheikh, rival fund managers sought to exploit my position by highlighting the unwanted political implications in which my activities had ensnared him.

The sheikh was eventually won over. With the loss of his investment, the company that I had spent years establishing crashed, almost overnight, to the ground. What followed was a period of unparalleled economic recession. All at once, my world had collapsed in ruin. Not a single pillar was left standing.

My first thoughts amidst all of this upheaval centred upon my wife and children: I had promised to provide them with a life of unbounded luxury, a life that would provide our children with an invaluable start and allow us all to live in comfort. But suddenly I was penniless, with more than a million pounds of unpaid debts to my name. What kind of life could I now provide for my wife and children?

Without work, and bereft of livelihood, the thoughts that had fermented within my subconscious for long and turbid years surfaced at the first sign of my idleness. It was not *I* that reflected on my life – but my *life* that reflected on me. It seemed to me as if I had always been suffering. My marriage and my unceasing efforts to make a living appeared as mere soporifics, sleeping-draughts, intended to dull the awareness of my essential nature. I had lived on the surface of my being; I had lived through my wife; never, though, had I had the courage to live as myself – *to be what I am.*

The crystallisation of numerous years of ignorance took shape in an instant. With breathtaking speed I finally glimpsed an awareness of the fact that I was a woman. It was impossible to ignore this knowledge. I questioned the direction of my life. What had I been searching for? For love? For money? For fame? As for fame and money, were they not merely means to an end – pursued in order to win my wife's love? And love? And my wife? Was my love for her anything but a blind grasping to live a substituted existence through a woman I regarded as perfect? The entire order of my existence had been turned on its head.

I was now 33 years of age. I felt compelled to enlighten my wife of the knowledge that I had gained. Unable to frame my dilemma in anything but clichés, I related every detail of my internal history to her, completing my narrative with a most ill-framed expression: that I believed *I was a woman trapped in a man's body*. The intimation I possessed that she was already aware of what I had related to her appeared to gain credence in both her lack of surprise and the understanding that she initially displayed. In retrospect, however, I believe that her reaction was more to be explained by the novelty of the situation than any semblance of understanding.

Straightaway she offered me the opportunity to dress myself in which ever clothes of hers I felt inclined; she initiated me into the glories of her dressing-table, investing me with the mysterious knowledge possessed only by women and make-up manufacturers! Our earlier discussions appeared as mere rehearsals to the evening which we then spent together, I dressed in female clothes and she treating me as another girl. After the experiences of the previous years, I thought that I had found the portal to a new source of happiness – one in which I could realise my true nature.

My hopes did not persist, however. My revelation was nothing less than *dynamite* – and it soon became apparent that I could not measure up to what was expected of a conventional husband. How utterly ridiculous to expect a spouse to come to terms with the knowledge that his or her partner is of the opposite sex than supposed!

My mind was not sufficiently clear to perceive the obvious consequences of my actions. Once the dust from the initial explosion had begun to settle, I found myself hopelessly inadequate to fulfil the role of a husband that any wife would expect. This loathsome disorder was a reproach; I suffocated in a perpetual stream of self-abuse. Forced into a corner, allowed no respite from the awareness of my problem, I lowered my head in shame for my very existence.

To release myself from the mental torment that I was experiencing, I decided to seek help, going first to my GP, who referred me to the Gender Identity Clinic at Charing Cross Hospital. But the year that I waited for an appointment heralded the collapse of our life together: the situation had become impossible. Except for that evening we spent together after I first told her about my problem, from the moment I unburdened myself of my feelings I had anticipated that my disclosure would eventually destroy our marriage.

Thus, when the situation finally became unendurable, I assented almost with alacrity to the prospect of divorce. My wife and I agreed to continue to live together, however, believing that it would be in the best interests of our children. But, assured that I would always possess the right to see our children whenever I needed, I was adamant in the belief that there existed no other way to resolve the insuperable difficulties our marriage presented.

*

The weeks that followed our divorce allowed us a certain degree of peace together. For me, the days were consumed with contemplating the direction that I would pursue, now that I was released from the sustaining influence of my ex-wife. But at the termination of my musings, I would always come up against the same thoughts. The future appeared to me an utter wilderness. It was all very well to contemplate my prospects and decisions while living in the home of my former wife and children – but would I not think differently if the time came when I had to depart, when my ex-wife found herself a new man?

On the surface, it appeared that nothing had happened. As if things had not changed in the slightest, I would make myself comfortable in my favourite armchair in the living room, with the children playing around me. But at once I would become aware of the difficulties the relationship between the two of us presented, and I would sink into the world of thought where my future seemed an utter wasteland.
For some time now I had secretly gathered information about my condition. Indeed, I had become aware of the

existence of transsexualism as a disorder, and the possibility of seeking its resolution in sex-reassignment surgery. If I had known about this years previously, the nature of my disorder would have become clear to me much earlier than it did. But shouldn't I have been aware, even in childhood, of the nature of my disorder? Shouldn't I have known, without a doubt, that I was really a girl? I was frustrated and despondent at these thoughts. How could someone like me, with a bristling moustache and masculine features, be transformed into a woman? Impossible!

For her part, my ex-wife remained extremely subdued, bearing with great fortitude the impossible situation my disorder had placed her in. She would spend more or less the entire day in front of the television, eating, and playing with her cats, as if nothing had happened. Surprisingly, the children appeared to be little disturbed by the situation. Their attitudes towards us had not altered in the least. Such was our life together, each of us coping with the situation as best we could.

My ex-wife would often go out to socialise, leaving me to take care of the children. She looked so beautiful – *a beauty redolent of the first time I saw her* – that I profoundly lamented I had let her go. I continued to love her to so great a degree, in fact, that I couldn't embody my feelings for her without uttering the most inadequate of words. Moreover, I became intensely jealous of anyone who might take possession of her beauty. Never could I conceive of breaking from my ex-wife – yet my only possibility of retaining her presence was to remain a witness to these spectacles of hopelessness. Whatever plans I had devised for the future were thrown aside, because I was so deeply embroiled in her activities.

Returning home from my office on a beautiful summer's day, I found my ex-wife's expression to be somewhat more anxious than usual. A feeling of utter emptiness pervaded my stomach, and my body flushed from head to toe. I knew what was coming, only I should have been better prepared for it. Faltering slightly, she explained the situation. She had met the "man of her dreams"; he was the chairman of a giant multi-national public company, and very rich.

Just before fainting you are sometimes aware of your senses closing down one by one. That was how I felt then. As she continued, my heart sank ever lower; and while she was eager to unburden herself of what was to all intents and purposes my death sentence, all I could think about was how my relationship with her and our children would be affected by these events.

*

For some time I was able to remain secretly with my ex-wife. I would have done anything to stay with her. Clutching at straws, I offered my services as driver and housekeeper. I resolved to remain on board even as I saw the ship sinking beneath the waves, ready to be crushed along with its timbers.

My ex-wife's new man became increasingly jealous of my relationship with his partner, and could not understand such a strange arrangement between ex-spouses. In an attempt to remain close to my ex-wife, I had been the first to suggest that she introduce me to her new lover. My intention had been simply to make friends with him and let him know I was in no way to be considered as a rival.

But this was not to be. The person that he finally met was not Sam Hashimi. What he saw was a caricature: a jealous husband fighting tooth and nail to retain at all costs his position as husband. Once he had taken in the situation, my position at home became untenable – and I was literally compelled to leave, finding myself at the wrong end of injunctions and legal proceedings.

*

I rented a little flat about half a mile from my children. There I remained, totally inert for days on end, staring aimlessly at the bare walls. I felt like an outcast, an abomination of nature, outside the realm of human sympathy. It would have been better for everyone if I had just ceased to exist! I found myself the object of reproach, rather than of pity. When the days of my life together with my ex-wife had almost reached their end, friends I met would tell me that I had brought all my troubles upon myself.

The natural course of day and night merged into one uncompromising chasm of darkness. Tears swirling forth from the cataract of my soul consumed my every hour. Pain, suffering, wakeful nights connecting the disjointed events of the day, all conspired to deny me the oblivion of sleep. From the depths of my endless tears I eventually lost all awareness of the time I remained, without stirring, perched on the settee in the living-room of my flat.

Still I continued crying. My tears seemed to echo against the empty walls. I needed help, or a friend to offer me solace – but not a single telephone call, not a visit from a single "friend", disturbed my lamentations. The days continued to pass, and still I could not release myself from my tears. The natural functions of my body had deserted me along with my friends. For days on end I could not eat. I felt that my life was slowly ebbing away from me – as if I was being released from a long period of torture.

"Could this be the end?" The thought that I was leaving this world, and my accursed body, descended upon me as a warm and friendly companion. Within the mosaic of my bewildered mind I dwelt upon the days I had spent living in a Buddhist commune in India. Buddha had taught that our only redemption was to escape from the body of clay that encases us;

that ultimate bliss resides in a state of Nirvana, in other words utter annihilation.

Stirring myself from my torpor, I weaved my way across the furniture of the room, coming to a halt in front of the medicine cabinet. An array of tablets (Temazepan, I think), seemingly aligned on parade, offered me their ministrations. Grasping handfuls of these, my allies, I made my way back to the settee. Lying down, I arranged my body in a comfortable position and swallowed the tablets. Drifting slowly into my final, all-embracing sleep, the pressing thought that I ought to leave a word for those who would find my body would not allow me to remain at rest. Lifting myself from the settee, I began to search for pen and paper. A disorientated blur clouded my mind and vision. Suddenly I collapsed, tumbling down onto the coffee-table, ornaments scattering across the floor. I was finally at peace.

The violence of my fall produced a loud crash, as my body thudded against the floor and the coffee-table shattered into a thousand pieces. Faces of curious neighbours pressed against the glass of the patio doors of the shared balcony. Someone called an ambulance. Police arrived and smashed the window. Unwillingly I was dragged back to life. Without a moment to spare, I was rushed to Ealing hospital and made to drink a thick black mixture of charcoal to dilute the effect of the tablets.

*

After recovering my health, I was diagnosed as clinically depressed and admitted to an Ealing psychiatric hospital, where I resided for the next four weeks. I had reached the nadir of existence: from the summit of wealth and fame I had plunged into unemployment, divorce, mental illness, and an attempt on my own life. But that was not all. Beneath this great matrix of problems, I knew that my gender disorder continued to persist.

Continuing to suffer from the shock of my attempted suicide and the effects that my gender disorder, I foolishly decided that I would contact my ex-wife, apologise for the past, and attempt to rebuild my life with her. Upon my discharge from hospital, I set my steps in the direction of my former wife's home, bounding with a delirious optimism and hope for the future. Not surprisingly, I soon found an application had been filed to have me committed to prison for harassment.

My position did not prove to be a particularly good defence against the onslaught of an array of expensive lawyers and advisers, and the support of my ex-wife's family. I stood alone, continuing to experience extended periods of depression, with neither a lawyer, an adviser, or a solitary family member to support me. Inevitably, I lost the case – and was even thankful to get away with a suspended prison sentence.

Over the months that followed I suffered no less than five consecutive mental breakdowns – each requiring extended periods of hospitalisation – and two separate stretches of imprisonment of three months' duration. I was too stupid to understand that I simply could not see my former wife and children any more.

Nineteen ninety-five was to be the worst year of my life.

Jailbird

I desperately needed to get away from the entire mess: away from Ealing, and away from my constant desire to gain access to my children. A day later, I was on my way to Thailand. Within a period of just two weeks I exhausted the entire Far East; not a single major city did I pass over in my attempt to rid myself of the treacherous thoughts that constantly sought to betray me into returning to my children. Just as on the day when I left the mental institution I had foolishly and against every dictate of reason returned to my ex-wife in the hope of rebuilding our relationship, so I now rushed headlong back to my children. Arriving back in London just two weeks after my initial departure, I returned to my flat to drop off my luggage.

On entering the flat, I found a message waiting for me on my answering machine – it was a message from my former wife, warning me to keep away from her and the children.

Without hesitation, I left my flat and within what seemed like a matter of seconds found myself at her house. She repeated the words she had uttered on the telephone. In response to my appeal to be enlightened of the reason for her statements, she explained that it would not be in anyone's best interests if I was allowed to see the children. But her resolution turned out to be far from steadfast. I had been there no more than a few minutes when a series of almost endless prevarications began. First she said that I couldn't see the children – then she changed her mind and said I could. "All right," she finally concluded, "you can take them ice-skating providing you get them back here before 6 o'clock." But it was now 4 o'clock. To take the children to Queensway (where the skating rink was) and back *and* have time for the skating itself, I would need at least until 7 o'clock.

I argued with her. I insisted the offer was impossible, it simply could not be done. Perhaps I was being pig-headed. After all, I could easily have suggested an alternative, less time-consuming, arrangement – but the only thing I could think of was that I possessed a natural right to see my children, and no one was going to get in the way of that. Eventually I lost control and hit her. It was unforgivable. Acting on first impulse, without pausing, I ran out of the house and arrived breathless back at my flat.

I heard nothing for the next two days. I was afraid and penitent. Given the terms of my previous suspended sentence, I feared that my ex-wife might bring a complaint against me. My suspicions proved correct. On the third day I was served with an order to attend Brentford County Court. Prison seemed imminent, and there was nothing I could do about it.

*

The Ford Transit rattled along with unremitting decisiveness towards my home for the next three months – Wormwood Scrubs. The naked steel of the little mobile prison, jolting and battering along the road, sent shocks of icy cold racing through my veins. Thirty minutes that seemed to last for ever brought the vehicle to a standstill. We had arrived. The massive prison gates swung back upon their hinges, and the Transit continued its journey; then, moments later, it halted outside the prisoners' reception. The doors of the van were flung open, and I was conveyed within the walls of the grim-looking Victorian fortress.

I found myself, along with 30 or 40 other unfortunates, in the prisoners' reception. The array of fierce and unfriendly faces, unceasingly surveying my person, frightened me. *It was me, Sam Hashimi, standing there – Sam, husband, and father of two*. Those around me seemed like so many murderers and thieves; they could never be fathers or husbands!

A loud and peculiarly institutional voice rose from amidst the tumult, calling my name. I followed the line of men that had preceded me. It was a pathway to degradation: my belongings were confiscated, I was photographed, stripped naked, and issued with the most repulsive items of apparel. Finally, my name was exchanged for a number. If earlier I had felt out of place among the convicts that surrounded me, I now became aware of how such differences are equalised – how convict and innocent are fused into one indissoluble whole.

There was one final step – the routine visit to the prison doctor – before I would find myself within the claustrophobic confines of a cell. Dr Rees was a sympathetic man. Probably he had come to recognise certain features and expressions among the prisoners he interviewed. Whatever the reason, he saw me as an individual who had ended up in the wrong place. "You shouldn't be in here," Dr Rees muttered, almost imperceptibly. He questioned me on the circumstances that had resulted in my incarceration. Regressing to the standard of my English 20 years previously, I spluttered out the catalogue of misfortunes that had landed me there. "Oh, one of those family stories!", the doctor exclaimed. "This wing will be far too harsh for someone like you. I'll arrange for you to be admitted to the prison hospital." My relief was quickly cut short – the hospital was full at present, I would be informed when a bed became vacant.

Walking unsteadily in the ill-fitting shoes I had been allocated, I was shown to my cell, in C Block. The door slammed shut behind me and I collapsed onto a mean plastic chair, mesmerised by the surreal atmosphere that pervaded the whole episode from start to finish. A bed as thin as a plank of wood, a toilet, and a rickety desk – this was my home. How could I reconcile this cell with my previous life? Was any of this really possible?

However deeply I searched the events that had led to this dungeon, in my disorientated state I could not draw any clear conclusion as to the acts which had provided the initial impetus in this whole strange affair. I had sought the fulfilment of a *natural right* – that of paternity – yet in doing so I had contravened the rights of my former wife and committed Contempt of Court. What was this strange contradiction of laws but a matrix in which my disorder made illegality seem inevitable? I had to free myself from this distorted world. Feelings similar to those which had preceded my earlier breakdown offered themselves as my only escape. They offered me friendship and a place to hide within myself: I accepted their embrace, and tears brought me solace.

At 5 o'clock the relative silence was shattered by the sound of cells being unlocked, and the cattle-like flock of noisy inmates making their way on to the landing of the block. My cell door was flung open: "Get y'self a plastic plate and mug, and some grub." If it had been possible, I would have stayed within the confines of my cell for the entire duration of my sentence. I did not want to communicate with the rough-looking characters I had glimpsed in the prisoners' reception. Realising that my life was no longer my own, I resigned myself and joined the noisy queue, all the time aware that they were staring intently at me, as I proceeded to the kitchens.

The infernal whispering didn't cease until I returned to my cell. "Wherever one is," I mused, "there is always a place one likes best!" – glad to be seated once again on that mean plastic chair. Just as I was recovering from my fright, a tiny rectangular flap in the door was lifted up. "Oy, Hashimi, come here!", commanded the voice of an inmate. Knowing that I would have to face this individual when the door was unlocked, I decided to obey his request. "Have you got any snout?", he asked. Not understanding this unusual term, I looked on in bewilderment. "Cigarettes!", he explained. "Sorry," I replied, "but I don't smoke."

I recognised a Moroccan accent. Arrested at Heathrow Airport while attempting to smuggle £5,000,000 of stolen jewellery out of the country, this young Moroccan boy, named Hamid, had attained a position among the elite inmates. He offered me a deal. In return for supplying him with twenty cigarettes a week (which I was to buy out of the £2.50 per week privilege I received as a civil prisoner – unlike my interlocutor, who was a criminal), I would be guaranteed absolute safety and a bunk within his own cell. Even before he finished speaking, he had found himself a deal! A moment later a prison officer approached, and ordered my benefactor to get on with his cleaning duties. Picking up his mop and bucket, Hamid continued on his way.

I passed a more or less restless night. Then, in the morning, a prison officer entered my cell and informed me that I had a visitor. My curiosity was stirred. "I haven't sent anyone a visiting order!", I blurted out. "Never mind that, follow me anyway." I was directed into a tiny room, perhaps even smaller than my cell. I waited an hour in complete silence – with no sign of any visitor. Eventually a key was forced into the door, and an officer announced that my visitor had arrived. He was a process-server sent by my ex-wife to serve some papers on me. Apparently I could not escape her even in prison! No, I was not going to put up with this, it was ridiculous. Why couldn't I be left alone? I refused to see my visitor.

I found I had spoken imprudently. I was informed in authoritative tones that I had no choice; that efforts to resist would be futile. Someone grabbed hold of my burgundy-coloured prison-issue pullover, and I was propelled into the adjoining room, landing on all fours. The process-server stood before me, grinning. Taking the injunction papers from his briefcase, he threw them at me, the papers cascading over my head and on to the floor. He then departed. Complaint was impossible – I concluded that I would have to bear such insults with the little fortitude I could muster.

*

A few days later, while in the showers, I was approached by an enormous brute of a fellow. By the menacing look on his face, I inferred that what he had to say would not be pleasant. "You've got beautiful lips – just like a woman. Do me a favour, Hashimi, put them round my penis." I was petrified; the thought sped through my mind that I was going to be raped. As he began to close in on me, I realised that my attempts to assuage his passion were proving utterly futile. I was more or less resigned to the worst.

From the depths of hopelessness, a way out of the situation revealed itself. Taking my final breath before I descended into oblivion, I saw my Moroccan friend approaching – I was saved. "I haven't seen you for a few days!", I cried. All at once my assailant knew his position was hopeless. A stern look from Hamid was enough to send him on his way.

At a cost of a mere 20 cigarettes a week, my investment proved to be remarkably good value. Not only did my Moroccan friend more than adequately provide the promised services. In addition, to possess a "bodyguard" who appeared so devoted to me gave the impression that I was a criminal of the first rank – no doubt extremely dangerous and inclined to explode at any moment.

The misconception the other inmates had constructed from a Moroccan boy and a few cigarettes never troubled me in the least. I had almost forgotten what it felt like to be respected. And if my fellow-prisoners were willing to accord me such an accolade, I saw no reason to stand in their way. That I was resident there because I had broken a court order to stay away from my wife and children – and not because I was a mass-murderer in for life – conveniently slipped my mind when anyone chose to question me on the subject!

Hospital

Dr Rees had not forgotten me. A bed became vacant in the prison hospital, and it was mine for the taking. I was allowed two minutes to stow my possessions into a black refuse sack, provided by a prison officer, before moving from my cell. Following the officer, I was led through a labyrinth of corridors, each separated by a heavy door. Through the prison exercise ground and along a little concrete path we continued, our journey coming to an end at the entrance to the hospital.

Prisoners from the C Block pressed their faces against the fence that partitioned the hospital from the rest of the prison. Among them Hamid, the Moroccan boy, yelled "Goodbye Hashimi, see you next time. Write to me when you're released – you can come and stay with me in Morocco!" The raucous hubbub of the inmates drifted into the background as I was finally led into the hospital building.

Within the hospital wing, the atmosphere was volatile. The inmates here were, for the most part, constituted of the severely mentally impaired and drug addicts, plus a few whose convalescence was of a purely physical nature. Surrounded by this array of "loose cannons", I wondered if I might have been better off staying where I was in C Block! Fully aware of the instability of the psychiatric patients, Dr Rees allocated me a cell among the physically ill, notwithstanding the fact that the grounds for my admittance – severe depression – were of a psychiatric nature.

Unlike C Block, in the hospital wing the most subdued silence persisted. Here one couldn't observe the cattle-like file of 500 inmates being decanted into the corridors. With neither exercise nor recreation, they remained locked in their cells for 23 hours each day, being released only for food and medication.

If one had deliberately sought the ideal conditions for intensifying one's depression, no better arrangements could have been found than those existing here. In this hot-bed of unhappiness I became increasingly depressed and introspective. Dr Rees did not fail to notice this. Interviewing me at one of our regular weekly meetings, he concluded: "I'm rather concerned about your condition. Taking account of what you've been through, it will hardly be to your benefit to remain here." A report was duly forwarded to my solicitor, suggesting that he appeal against my sentence on medical grounds.

Two days later Mr Sankhla, my solicitor, came to see me. His face radiated with confidence. I was to appear before a judge at the High Court in London; it should be a simple affair – all that was required was that I apologise to both the judge and my ex-wife. I would surely then be released.

Once again I was transported across London – this time in a sturdy and systematically arranged vehicle. Like a miniature battery-farm on wheels, it consisted of a mass of tiny cubicles, abutting one another like a row of upright coffins. In one on these cells I found myself handcuffed, conveyed, and delivered to the High Court. Shuffled out of the vehicle, I was then chained and dragged through the entrance, before being delivered to the court room where my appeal was to take place.

It was a farce. My ex-wife's barrister requested that my appeal be denied. His request was soon accepted by the Court. In next to no time I was back in the prison hospital, before I'd even had a chance to reflect on the matter. Dr Rees and the consultant from Ealing hospital were outraged: this was appalling, and should not be tolerated! They at once sent a report to the Home Secretary giving details of my case. That same day I found myself ferried back to Ealing hospital, in time for dinner. Six weeks later I was released.

*

Walking slowly and hesitantly along the roadside, with my refuse sack of belongings slung over my shoulder, I trudged along aimlessly, not knowing where to go. I possessed neither a home, money or food, and I was without a friend in the world.

My ambling finally brought me to the house which I once shared with my wife and children. Opposite the magnificent expanse of Walpole Park, it stood proudly, tyrannically, as if it had never seen or heard of Sam Hashimi. As I encircled the park, an involuntary smile played across my lips, expressing remembrance of a life once so joyful. I couldn't resist taking a closer look at my former family home. No sign of life was visible. Moving closer, I pressed my face against the windows: no one remained. Collapsing on the steps with exhaustion, I could no longer restrain my tears. The emptiness that pervaded this once so happy home reflected the emptiness of my heart.

For now, I had to find a place to stay, at least for the night. I considered sleeping underneath the trees in Walpole Park – perhaps it would help me to come to terms with the shock I had undergone in finding my old home deserted. No, it was November, and the frost was already beginning to penetrate the worn soles of my shoes and up into my legs. Whether I cared to live or not, freezing to death struck me as being one of the most unpleasant ways to leave the world.

I made my way to Ealing YMCA. After experiencing great difficulty gaining entrance – a wrangle over cash at the door almost resulted in my forced departure – the porter agreed to allow me one month's residence, until Christmas of 1995.

There appeared to be very little difference between my present accommodation and that of the recent past. Even the residents of the two institutions were similar. Once again my table companions were drawn from life's unfortunates: alcoholics, drug addicts, and those who were just down on their luck. It was like being back in the prison hospital.

Some days later I received a letter. Apparently my whereabouts was not unknown to everyone; my ex-wife's solicitor was onto to me again. A neighbour had seen me circling my old home, and followed up her surveillance by reporting my presence to my ex-wife's solicitor. Contained in his letter was the assertion that my actions constituted "harassment", and that further such behaviour would result in my return to prison. A strange state of affairs indeed! I was on the receiving end of injunctions, threats of imprisonment, and summonses – and yet I was the one who was supposed to be carrying out the harassment. I could not come to terms with such a nightmarish arrangement of things.

Christmas found me still at the YMCA. Like so many other lonely people, I spent Christmas day on my own; ate Christmas dinner on my own; and saw the close of Christmas day on my own. During this lonely period it was only the thought of one day seeing my children again that sustained me. Foolishly, I hoped that love would overcome the obstructions that the law had placed before me; that it was inevitable that my desire would one day be fulfilled.

In response to continual requests, my solicitor had promised to persist in attempting to arrange access to my children, demanding that in the meantime I "pull my socks up". This was sound advice. Whatever the future might have in store, it would not go against my case to be seen carving out a new life for myself, in spite of the difficulties with which I was confronted.

I made a New Year's resolution: never again would I return to hospital, or to prison. The coming year, 1996, would initiate a period of profound self-inspection – Sam Hashimi and his body would, metaphorically, be placed under the microscope. I knew that beneath the numerous layers of my existence the woman who had so often demanded realisation continued to persist, and that the time was approaching for her birth into this world. *This time she would not be suppressed.*

In a vast converted warehouse in West London a New Year's Eve party of unparalleled proportions was being held. Among two thousand inebriated revellers I celebrated my new hope – *Samantha's new hope* – and, as I pondered upon her coming into being, I danced and kissed the community of hope that saw in the coming year cause for celebration. I danced until the daylight demanded my submission to nature herself.

Ascent

On January 2nd I returned to my doctor to find out whether any progress had been made with my application to Charing Cross Gender Clinic. As usual, I was informed that it would be at least another year before an appointment was likely to become available. "I'm desperate," I argued. "Couldn't the process be speeded up?" "Everyone who comes to see me with a request to consult Mr Montgomery is desperate," the doctor replied. "I'm afraid you are going to have to wait your turn."

Utterly despondent, I tried to think of other means of obtaining help. Waiting for the National Health Service was useless. "At least a year," the doctor had said. What did "at least" mean? It could mean a year; then again, it could mean five years. This was no good at all. On the other hand, even if I happened to receive an appointment tomorrow, what could the National Health Service do for me? First, they would attempt to dissuade me from the course of action I desired to undertake; and if they did accept the necessity for it, at best they would provide me with a trial course of hormones and send me away. But was that enough? Would they help me remove the bristling moustache perched over my lips? Would they provide me with a replacement for my unwieldy nose, or arrange for the provision of breasts? Undoubtedly, they would not.

There was only one possible way to obtain professional help: money. (And professional help would not finally be attained until the experience of falling in love had once again distracted me from the goal I had set myself.) "I was foolish not to have attended to the problem when I could have afforded the treatment," I mused. "But then I was married with two children. It would have been impossible..."

My thought process was brought to a halt. First of all, it had been fear and respect for my parents that had obstructed the realisation of Samantha, then my love for my wife and children, and now lack of money. Had I always been searching for a reason to evade myself? "No more...", I concluded. "No more will I play the part of a craven coward, hiding behind excuses. I will find a means to obtain the money. I will make money, and I will become Samantha. It is as simple as that."

Confident that I had hit on plans to get my life in order, I was aware that my most immediate need was to depart from my present residence in the YMCA. It was impossible to achieve anything while living under such conditions. Surveying the past, I realised that my supposition that I was completely destitute of friends had been incorrect. There were numerous individuals who would be willing to offer me a helping hand – first-class people with whom I had become acquainted with during my period in the football industry. I decided to give one such individual a call.

Reg Brealey answered the telephone himself. "Sam, what's happened to you? I haven't heard from you in ages." Overjoyed to hear the voice of someone who had once shown such friendship and support, I felt my life had already begun an ascent towards brighter days. I related the events of the past years, describing each precisely. My words could not have fallen upon more understanding ears. "Sam," he began, "You don't have a worry in the world. You still possess a great business mind. You have numerous business contacts in the Middle East. And, most importantly, you have your health." Within the hour he had provided me with a ticket to the Middle East, and enough money to keep me going for the time being. His plans for me were summed up in a single sentence: "Get on the plane and do some business!" I owe my life to Reg.

*

Within the confines of a modern air-conditioned office block located within an affluent suburb of Amman, contracts were exchanged and a deal was made. A Jordanian property company was intent on expanding its activities to London; they needed someone who possessed the necessary business and artistic abilities. The first of their new projects was the refurbishment of a luxury apartment in Park Lane. The "someone" was to be Sam Hashimi, and this property was to be my home for the next six months. I returned to London on the first available flight. The money I so desperately needed was to be mine!

After six gruelling months, the Park Lane apartment was ready. Following a number of further refurbishment projects, I arrived at a three-storey house in Kensington, which was the location of my next assignment. The door was opened by an Israeli lady with a warm and friendly smile. Such an expression I had not encountered for years. I returned her smile, and we went into the house to discuss the nature of the work she required.

While exchanging ideas relating to the design of her property, I noticed that beneath her overtly determined and businesslike manner there existed a source of enduring sadness. I recognised this sadness – it was quite unmistakable, as each species of sadness is distinct from another. "Here is a woman", I pondered, "who has undergone the heartache of separation." My supposition proved correct. Six years had not been sufficient to loose the bonds of loneliness. Neither money, nor travel, nor lovers had succeeded in dissipating her "ghostlike existence" – which was how she herself referred to her life.

Between us a bond of sympathy and love developed with lightning rapidity, and the weeks that followed heralded the coming of my second marriage. Together we formed a successful team, launching a property and finance business. Apart from her vast financial assets, she had been the owner of a well-known company that boasted royal personages among its clients. Moreover, I had accumulated considerable capital from my work in property design. Our lifestyle was thus one of great opulence. Between us, we bought a brand-new Rolls Royce "Silver Spirit" and transformed our home into one of palatial magnificence.

Whether it is true that the events in life revolve in a circle, I cannot say – but the prosperity that I had experienced in the past featured again in my new life. In addition, as if existence had not yielded sufficiently of her treasures, I obtained a Court ruling stating that I was to be allowed supervised contact with my children. I had become a friend of life once more.

For the first time in a year I saw my children, and our conversation was so happy and bright that I believed there was nothing further that life could offer me. The children's grandfather was present, gossiping amiably with my new wife. Together we must have presented an idyllic picture, and a gesture of goodwill between the children's grandfather and myself concluded what had been a quite overwhelming reunion.

When I awoke next morning, I could not believe that the events of the previous day had actually occurred. Had I imagined all this? Or perhaps it had been a dream? My anxiety was rapidly dissipated, however. Lying beside me, my wife dispelled my misgivings and confirmed that the reunion with my children hadn't been a figment of my imagination. Furthermore, she told me we were to leave the following morning for the Seychelles, our honeymoon destination.

*

After our return from the Seychelles our marriage soon started to deteriorate. Apart from residing for a whole year with building work continually going on around us, differences over share-ownership in our business began to cause arguments between us. In addition, the second supervised visit to my children turned out to be a surprisingly dissatisfying event. As previously, my ex-wife's father was present – but this time I did not get on with him. Even the children were miserable, and the atmosphere was highly strained.

Certain financial settlements between myself and my first wife remained outstanding. My second wife was on to the matter like a shot. Lawyers, banks, advisers – all the paraphernalia of court cases were at once back on the scene. The immediate result was that my ex-wife found herself compelled to pay a substantial sum back to bank; I found myself back in court, once again extricating myself from the threat of prison; and access

to my children was again withdrawn.
Within a period of six months my second wife and I had separated. I did not see her again until the time when I received a letter requesting that I attend Court in connection with the nullification of our marriage. By then I had already progressed some way along the path to womanhood; and so, no doubt imprudently, I attended the Court dressed as a female.

In Court my second wife was asked to take the stand first. However, before she had a chance to speak, the judge broke in with "I'm sorry madam, but the proceedings will have to be adjourned until your husband is present." She and I looked at one another in bewilderment. There was I, sitting right in front of the judge, and yet he couldn't see me! Had I become invisible? "But my husband is in Court," my wife replied. All at once everything became clear. Perched on the edge of his seat, surveying the room vigorously, once again the judge declared "I cannot proceed unless your husband is present." He had taken me for a woman. "But he is present!", my wife replied, gesturing towards me. The judge realised that the case was conclusive – and, looking extremely diffident, pronounced the annulment.

The emergence of Samantha.

Bye-bye Sam, Hello Samantha!

Obviously I was not quite cut out for conventional married life. The experiences of the last 13 years had taught me *that*, if nothing else. Yet there was something else: for some time I had been possessed of the knowledge that, beneath the external existence of Sam Hashimi, Samantha was awaiting her turn to experience the light of day. At 37 years of age, I felt that I might not have another opportunity to initiate the process of sex-reassignment. I therefore resolved that all my efforts would now be directed to the fulfilment of this end.

After the termination of my second marriage, I rented a small one-bedroom flat in Kensington. Alone, I was able to do whatever I pleased with utter impunity. I was still undecided about how I was going to obtain professional treatment. For the time being, I decided to alter my appearance by those means that were available to me – such as plucking my eyebrows, removing my body hair, and having my nails manicured. At this early stage I also decided to permanently remove my facial hair by electrolysis.

While perusing a copy of *The Tranny Guide* earlier in December, I had noticed the address of a consultant psychiatrist named Russell Reid. The information given about his practice promised to provide me with both psychological and practical solutions to my gender problems. Up to then I had allowed this information to remain dormant, tucked away at the back of my mind – even to the extent of more or less forgetting its existence entirely. Perceiving that there was no other direction open to me, I abandoned Charing Cross once and for all, and decided that the time had finally come to pay Dr Reid a visit.

*

Anyone who has never ventured into a gender clinic (and few people have!) will probably be curious to know what one is likely to find. Perhaps many of my readers will therefore forgive me if I describe the inhabitants and nature of the clinic in some detail.

If you happen to pass a little shop displaying fruit and vegetables and notice a flight of steps immediately to your right, it is possible that you may have stumbled upon the surgery of Dr Russell Reid. Let us take a look inside and see what we can find. Descending the steps, you will immediately notice a radical change in atmosphere. From the warm and often breezy pathway that takes you to this cleavage in the earth, you are confronted with a dense, heavy atmosphere, cold with the misery of all who venture there. Follow me while I lead you into the clinic.

Uneven moss-covered paving slabs lead you to the entrance of this secret establishment, this freemasonry of nature's damned. It is a fearful moment. Behind, there is nothing but cavernous grey walls, criss-crossed with ivy; in front, a huge blue door of almost massive proportions. You proceed, trembling, towards this veritable portal. All of a sudden an unnerving clang rises from below. No need to worry, though – you have merely rearranged the array of beer cans that lie, carelessly discarded, along the shingle border.

Enough of this, Dr Reid is waiting! The doorbell is on the left. Do not hesitate now, a single buzz and your expectations will be satisfied. Clunk! The latch has fallen back, a single push and the door opens, one might say almost "invitingly". A vision of restrained and curious anxiety greets you. But there is no time to take in the sights yet – the receptionist awaits your credentials. Hers is the only clearly illuminated section of the room. Placed in bold relief against the subdued light, the secretary – the finished product, as it were – is carefully arranged for viewing. A canopy of light radiates from this corner, a light reflecting the hopes and aspirations of the occupants of this forlorn community.

She will ask you to take a seat. Turning 180 degrees back toward the door, you are confronted for the first time with the clinic in its entirety. Settees are dotted around the room. There is one particularly well suited to the taller transsexual, allowing the greater part of the heftier visitor's extended frame to sink into the swamplike embrace of the cushions; and one for the self-confident – hard and rigid, like a prison bed. Those who would choose to place their posterior among these unfriendly cushions must adopt an expression somewhat akin to that of the distinguished "veteran" proudly seated at the reception desk of the clinic!

As you evaluate the topography, you will inevitably become aware that there is a hierarchical arrangement. Facing the door, in clockwise sequence, beginning with the left couch and terminating with the receptionist, three species can be distinguished: the hopeless, those endowed with feline complacency and, last of all, the blithely supercilious.

Don't be in too much of a rush. Tea and coffee await. Just help yourself – the milk is in the refrigerator and the sugar on the side. Oh, and you can find yourself a mug in the cupboard above the sink. As you absent mindedly pour yourself a cup of tea so as not to seem impolite, a curious phenomenon gradually becomes evident. Behind the magazines which the individual occupants of the clinic seem to be so interested in reading, pairs of eyes pop up here and there – like periscopes – snatching furtive glances at each other! Even those glumly slouched on the left couch cannot resist sneaking the occasional glance. As you catch a glimpse of the incumbents of that particular couch, the reason for the magazines becomes all too evident!

Seated among this compendium of nature's chimeras, you will be better able to study each of the occupants with greater exactness. How vast the chasm of hope that separates these beings! One by one, as their names are called out, they have no option but to expose their erect figures before the eyes of all present. One individual, perhaps seven foot in height, draws a huge expanse of body from the settee. This great brute doggedly places one foot unhappily in front of the other as he crosses the faded beige carpet – years spent fighting aimlessly against the wrath of nature, but to no avail! Another individual, perhaps, of small yet stocky stature, graced with a heavily stubbled face, bald head and prominent features, stands up when the name "Rebecca" is called. A third – a business man in a pin-striped suit, smart black leather briefcase clasped tightly in hand – makes his way shamefacedly, almost as if involuntarily, to the door of Dr Reid's consulting room. This poor brute will see his life ruined overnight. A sad sight indeed!

All is not for the worst, however. Among the poor creatures we have just seen in the waiting room of the clinic, there are one or two individuals, like diamonds encrusted in a lump of coal, who have run the gauntlet,

Samantha. One of the diamonds?

who have endured the hardships, and finally emerged as attractive, sometimes even beautiful, women. A glorious sight indeed! These are the individuals that you will occasionally encounter in your everyday life, without ever knowing they were once men. You will see them – but in another sense you will *never* see them. In the supermarket, buying the week's groceries, in the office, even at the head of a large company – do not doubt it, they are everywhere.

...But we have tarried long enough in the clinic. Dr Reid has patients to see, and it is high time we returned to our narrative.

*

Russell Reid confirmed the nature of my disorder as the transsexual syndrome. Leaving his surgery with prescription in hand, I dashed to the chemist to obtain the female hormones I had been prescribed. At last, after all those years of waiting, within the palm of my hand I held the key to womanhood! I was elated. Now it was time to pursue Samantha in earnest.

*

During this period I continued to work in property design. But I soon noticed that an imperceptible change of attitude was slowly becoming evident among my business associates. Previously I was looked upon as any other business person. I would participate in their conversations; lunch with them; and work together on mutual projects.

Their initial reaction towards the minor transformations they noted in my appearance had been one of jest. It was presumed that I had undergone the various beauty treatments "for a laugh". It was not long, however, before they realised that I was serious about these matters. At that point, a collective distancing became evident among my associates. No longer did my position as "one of the boys" possess any validity. I had gradually undergone a transition to "outsider". Though I could understand their difficulty in coming to terms with what I was going through, I often felt they could perhaps have been a little more willing to overcome their fear of the situation. Not surprisingly, they felt uncomfortable continuing to work with me; they didn't need this additional problem. In the end, I felt it would be better for everyone if I left. I was a nuisance, an embarrassment to them.

Offers of joint commissions soon began to dry up. No one was willing to undertake projects in conjunction with me. It was pointless to continue. I had to accept the inevitable – the need to be myself was going to mean the loss of my business.

However, these events did not result in too great a setback for me. I'd accrued enough money to provide both for my livelihood and for the alterations that were necessary if I was to succeed in becoming a woman. In addition, my freedom helped me escape the abuse that I encountered when in public places. During the initial stages of my sex change I experienced a great deal of unpleasantness. I had not anticipated the response of people in the street. Perhaps a little optimistic in my beliefs, I had imagined they would somehow realise I was suffering from a gender disorder and that, if anything, they would be inclined to treat me with sympathy. But not so. The slightest deviation from the norm and curious individuals were onto me like a shot. Whether it was my nails or the shape of my eyebrows, not a single anomaly went unnoticed.

As I walked down the street people would glance at me and, with furtive grins, whisper some hidden insult to one another. Others would not be so demure in their abuse. As if it was incumbent on them to bring such anomalies to everybody's attention, they would, at the top of their voice, remark "He's wearing make-up!" or "That's a man!" And, fitting me into what appeared to be the most obvious category, as often as not they would conclude that I was homosexual. There seemed to be no rational explanation why these people found it necessary to announce their discovery to everyone else; even the most reticent individuals would audibly inform the world of my strange appearance.

In many ways, those early days were not dissimilar to the life of a convicted criminal. Sometimes afraid to leave the house for fear of insults, I experienced what was tantamount to a period of house arrest. It was a period of twilight reconnoitres (it was easier after dark to hide my affliction); of fear of being attacked by late-night revellers; of repeatedly crossing and recrossing the road when courage flagged and eye refused to meet eye in common contempt. All this seemed more akin to the existence of an escaped convict than someone who was suffering – and suffering greatly – from a congenital disorder.

My resolution was in no way diminished by these difficulties. Rather, I felt impelled to get through this transitional period as quickly as I could and, in every way possible, to speed it up. I was now approximately three months into the period of feminisation, and my features had noticeably altered. But ultimately I could do nothing but patiently wait for these changes to become fully effective with the passage of time.

However, this was not the case with other aspects of my body that I knew needed to undergo radical change. The money I had saved during my time spent in property design could be used to pay for such changes without delay. The only difficulty was deciding where to begin, so numerous were the obvious defects in my appearance. Should I attend first to replacing the tiny breasts that the female hormones had produced with prosthetic implants? Should I have the unsightly gaps in my teeth fixed? Or should I modify my unwieldy male nose by means of rhinoplasty? The list seemed endless. At 37 years of age, masculinity had become so securely entrenched in my appearance that it would be extremely difficult to eradicate it. Yet, for all that, over the following months I underwent so much surgery that I finally succeeded in eliminating these elements of masculinity.

Three months into the course of hormone therapy, I found myself approaching the next important juncture in my progression towards womanhood. Up till now it had been impossible for me, in public, to wear the clothes appropriate to my prospective sex. Since I still continued to retain certain indefinable elements of my former masculine self, it would have been highly imprudent to walk to the corner shop sporting a skirt or dress! I therefore found myself constrained to adopting an androgynous appearance, identifiable neither as male or female. On one occasion, however, it had been necessary to shake the moths from my masculine wardrobe.

I was standing before the mirror in the living-room of my Kensington flat applying some make-up, when the telephone rang. Picking up the receiver, I recognised the voice of Peter, a lawyer I had first met some years earlier while on business in Monte Carlo. Discovering a mutual interest in business, we had since sustained intermittent telephone communication, during which we would discuss business deals of massive proportion, projects that would shake the very foundations of the world economy. I say "discuss" as our projects never amounted to more than words.

Infused with his usual unquenchable enthusiasm, Peter gabbled away. "Sam, what's happened to you, dear boy? Where have you been? I haven't seen you for ages!" In response to this fusillade of questions, I went on the offensive by putting up a barrage of hot air. But my feeble excuses were impatiently brushed aside, and all attempts to extricate myself from the situation were in vain. "Nonsense!", he gushed. "What absolute poppycock! I simply must see you today. I'll meet you at the Dorchester for lunch." With this Peter, and his ebullience, abruptly disappeared.

What should I do? Meet him for lunch as planned, introducing myself, a woman, as Sam Hashimi? No, that wouldn't do. I would either have to attend in the guise of a man or not at all. Adopting the former course, I commenced the process of transformation – this time from woman to man. So, I removed my make-up, tied back my hair and, donning my discarded male attire, left for lunch.

As I entered the Dorchester Hotel, I was immediately conscious of being the centre of attention. Everyone peered at me with covert glances, as if I was some kind of strange and exotic creature. What exactly the lunch-time drinkers at the Dorchester said to one another that day I will of course never know – but my lunch with Peter, who was among the dumbfounded, gave me some fairly strong clues.

"You look different. Can that really be you, Sam?",

asked Peter. I suddenly had profound misgivings about what might follow. Determined not to inform him of the real cause of the now obvious changes that my appearance had undergone, I prepared myself for a silence that could utter no lies.

I kept my eyes firmly directed towards my glass while Peter initiated the usual commonplaces of lunch-time conversation. However, he quickly brought himself to a standstill and, adopting an inquisitive yet apologetic expression, leaned across the table and said "Sam, may I ask you a question?" I replied in the affirmative and, without further preamble, he continued "Do you pluck your eyebrows?" Following a simple "yes" from me, he said "Tell me, are you getting into the rock music business?" Although I couldn't see any obvious connection between rock music and plucked eyebrows, I was only too pleased to procure a façade for my apparently strange appearance, so I quickly replied "Of course. How ever did you guess!"

This seemed to appease Peter's inquisitiveness for the moment – but a few minutes later I was aware of that same inquisitive yet apologetic glance, followed by an embarrassed pause. "Oh no, here comes yet another question!", I thought. "Do you manicure your nails?" I reverted to Peter's own explanation. Then I noticed that he was staring intently at my face. My defences were rapidly crumbling. "Your face looks like a woman's!", he said. All I could do was give a feeble smile and remain silent.

I let him rattle on for the next hour. Needless to say, however, just before my departure, he could not resist a final question which reduced my remaining defences to ruins. "Are you growing breasts?" Unable to produce, even from the most uncharted depths of the labyrinth of my imagination, a plausible explanation for the protuberances in my shirt, I hastily said goodbye and dashed out of the hotel. I never did see Peter again.

*

The time had now come for me to stow away my male clothes once and for all among the moths and dust of the wardrobe, and face the "important juncture" I mentioned earlier – that of publicly adopting the role of a woman. What this expression signifies is the permanent adoption of female clothes and mannerisms; in short, living as a regular female lives. But it is very difficult to adopt female characteristics without first dressing as a woman full-time; accordingly, I removed the dust cover from my female wardrobe.

On that day I resolved to confront the world with the announcement of *who I am...* No longer would I be compelled to live the life of an actor, to live the two-tiered existence of a woman hiding behind the façade of a man. I studied myself in the mirror. The fact was unmistakable: I was now looking more feminine than I had ever done before.

A question that exercised me greatly was exactly how I should bring about these transformations. Precisely what makes a face female? Indeed, what makes a face male? The eyes? The nose? The lips? Or, rather, does the answer reside in seeking the sex in the entirety, the complete composition of the face? I pondered further the question of discovering which element, taking the human body in its entirety, plays the central role in the respective sex-determination of man and woman. The question no doubt seems absurd. Who, indeed, would cite any part of the body other than the genitals in answer to this question?

Yet, to bluntly assert that gender and genitalia are interchangeable terms overthrows the entire question of transsexualism. The majority of people belong to the gender expressed by the genitalia they happen to be born with. But I saw quite the contrary both in myself and in other transsexuals who I encountered. I saw the mind begging the individual for recognition, for self-expression through the body, *in* the body, *to become embodied…* I saw entire lives bolstered down with adamantine rivets; children loved so tenderly torn from a parent who could no longer live the life of an actor; bankruptcy, fortunes swallowed up overnight, the work of a lifetime squandered, when the mind no longer would be suppressed. What had not been sacrificed to transsexualism!

Such thoughts as these only served to intensify my perplexity. Whatever the outcome, I concluded that before me stood either a woman or, at worst, a very peculiar-looking man. My skin felt softer to the touch; my entire face had adopted a more relaxed expression; the coarseness of my beard had decreased considerably, due to the all too extended sessions of electrolysis that I had undergone. There was simply no denying it, I was becoming a woman.

All woman!

The Operation

Although the social ambiguity of the earlier stages of the sex-change process had been tormenting, from the date when I adopted the female role I noticed a gradual yet unmistakable increase in my ability to pass as an ordinary woman. It was sometimes difficult to monitor this gradual change over the days and weeks that passed; but there was absolutely no doubt about it, my transition would soon be complete.

With the approval of Dr Reid, it was agreed that, providing I was adamant in my decision, I could seek consent to proceed with the operation to reconstruct my genitals. Before such an operation can take place, it is necessary to secure two separate sources of consent. The first had been provided by Dr Reid; the other would require a trip to Brighton to see a certain Dr Dalrymple.

The weather in Brighton was filthy, the entire coastline one great quagmire of mud. Rain fell in torrents.

Perched on a bleak hill, the hospital sat upon one vast blanket of water-drenched grass.

Arriving at the main entrance, I made my way through numerous almost identical corridors, finally emerging outside Dr Dalrymple's office. As I sat and glanced at the entrance to the room housing the man who was to decide my future, thoughts concerning the gravity of what I was undertaking kept on filtering through my mind. Was I absolutely sure I wanted to go ahead with the operation? The extensive surgery I would have to undergo and the pain that would follow bothered me greatly – and I felt deeply distressed at the thought of severing this final bond of paternity with my children. I still passionately desired access to my children, and I feared that such surgery might prejudice my case.

For the first time, I felt some degree of hesitation over the course of action I was taking. I needed to hear from my children themselves. Taking up a pen and paper, I wrote the following note and sent it, along with Christmas presents, to my children:

> *To my dear children,*
>
> *I want you to know how much I love you, and how much I miss you. Please don't be angry with me any longer. I know that you may still be upset with me, but even grown-ups do stupid and foolish things sometimes, which they may regret afterwards.*

But especially at this time of year we all must forgive each other and forget the bad things, and only remember the good times we had together.

My only wish now that I am on my own is to hear from you from time to time, just to tell me how you are, and to hear some happy things about your life.

If you can send me a letter sometime and maybe even a photograph of you, that would be wonderful.

Once more, my dear daughter and my dear son, I want you to know that you are part of me and that I love you very much.

Sam
xxxxxx

My letter went unanswered.

Reflecting on what the future might hold in store, I perceived ahead of me nothing but a wilderness of solitude. I had suffered tremendously living the life of a man. *But what of that?* Would not life without my children be unbearable? I felt that I would be prepared to abandon my plans of physically becoming a woman if there was a chance of re-establishing communication with them. But that was not to be.

I found it impossible to remain idle at such a time. During the days that preceded the operation, both day and night, I wandered the unfriendly streets, seeking some scrap of solace amidst the bustling crowds. The sorrow I experienced had made me a lonely outcast; and my aimless wandering only served to intensify my despondency.

I was taunted by the advent of Christmas. All around, parents were looking for those special presents that would fill their children's faces with joy. Usurping the accustomed dominance of their parents, they drag their weary mothers and fathers into every toy shop they chanced to pass. The repeated image of Father Christmas, the brightly coloured lights, the jollity percolating through the family triangle... Were my children among such happy revellers? How much more of this would I have to endure? The very events that had once yielded so much happiness became the bane of my existence.

Exiled from my children, engulfed in a heavy grey cloud – and that solitary hospital overlooking a choppy sea that swept down from the hospital – I felt totally alone. Without a doubt, these turbid waters could have received my body, and not a word of sadness would have been communicated to my children. Not knowing – perhaps not even able to comprehend – the nature of my disorder, my ceasing to exist would have been, literally, a drop in the ocean.

*

A new urgency had thus arisen. My children, though torn asunder in exile, were yet inexorably linked to me by a single thread – by the fact of my being their father. If I was to sever that link by resorting to surgery, would not my children be lost forever? Legal advice confimed my suspicions: at that time and given the circumstances of the case, proceeding with surgery would have been tantamount to ending any chance I might have had of ever seeing my children again. This was the dilemma – to retain the meagre vestige of hope that remained of gaining further access to my children (a hope that would possibly never come to fruition), or go ahead with surgery and cast my last hope into the abyss?

Hours, days, weeks passed, and not a single word did I receive from my children. As a condemned criminal awaits the hangman, hoping against hope that a word from a silent witness may free him, so did I await word from my children – some tiny ray of hope that would secure my redemption. But no word came. Taking from the drawer beside me photographs of my little boy and girl, I placed them to my lips and kissed them. A solitary tear fell from my eyes. Then, no longer able to restrain the unceasing, eternal suffering forced upon me, a torrent welled up and spilled from my eyes. I cried; I cried profusely; I cried until my broken heart anticipated its departure from this world. "Goodbye my children. So brief the time since last we were together, playing, laughing, and embracing in the warm confines of love. Never will a single moment of our time together ever leave me. Love, eternal in endurance, will draw us together once again. And if this life should force us apart, beyond the grave we shall find salvation."

On December 17th, a cold snowy day, I packed my case and departed for the hospital.

*

I duly arrived at the hospital without any misgivings concerning the surgical procedure that I was about to undergo. The question of my children had even generated in me a kind of complacency. Their absence seemed to have made me impervious to the physical pain that was to follow; nothing could hurt me anymore.

Helping me with my luggage, a nurse directed me to the lift that would take me to the second floor where my room was located. "Is there anything you need?" she asked in that affable manner peculiar to nurses. When I answered in the negative, she departed. I sat on the bed and looked around me. A regular private room: a bed, remote-control television, a buzzer for assistance – I could have been there for anything.

"This little room is to be my home for the next 10 days," I mused. "And this bed could easily become my tomb!" I walked over towards the window. The outlook was dreary. Beneath the grey, overcast sky, the soggy fields stretched towards the sea. In the background I could hear the voices of nurses ministering to patients, their footsteps marching to the orders of a busy schedule, and the occasional din of a neighbouring television. So much was going on around me, tucked away in this little room. Slowly and in a subdued manner I unpacked my case, stowing my clothes in the wardrobe and my books and magazines on the bedside cabinet that would be the limit of my world while I recovered from the operation.

The nurse soon returned. Perched upon the edge of the bed, she informed me that I could have nothing more to eat this side of the operation – "Nothing but water." From her hand she produced two or three sachets of a white powdery substance: laxatives to clear the contents of my bowels before the operation. The nurse left. Within half an hour I found myself glued to the lavatory, without respite, for virtually the whole of the afternoon. By 9 o'clock that evening I was asleep.

After a surprisingly good night's sleep (probably due to naivety concerning what awaited me) I was informed that Mr Royle, the surgeon, would be coming to see me later that morning. My stomach felt empty; I was thirsty; nervous - it was really going to happen. Never before had the imminence of my sex change struck me so profoundly. It would take just four hours of surgery to transform me into a woman! Strangely reassuring in my moment of anxiety, the television hummed away monotonously on the other side of the room, oblivious to these events. Everything would be all right.

Ten-thirty brought Mr Royle to my room. A tall man in his late fifties, with grey-brown slicked back hair and sporting a pin-striped suit, he was one of those figures that radiate an authority tempered with friendliness and understanding. He smiled warmly and sat down on the chair beside my bed. "Well Samantha," he proceeded, "how are you feeling?" "I'm fine," I replied. "You're aware of the procedure of the operation, and what it entails. If you're certain that this is what you want, we are ready to go ahead." I nodded in assent. "Well, so long as you understand that the procedure is irreversible, we will be operating at 12 o'clock today." "I don't possess any doubts – I'm sure this is what I want." "Good luck, then. I'll see you in the theatre this afternoon." And with one of his inimitable smiles, he left the room.

As the time for the operation drew nearer, I became more relaxed – or, rather, more resigned to it. I had awaited this moment so eagerly, for so long. Indeed, looked at objectively, it was a blessing that a disorder of the kind I was suffering from could be corrected by surgical means.

When Mr Royle had gone, a nurse handed me a battery shaver to clear hair from the site of surgery. I grasped this instrument as if it was a symbol of the knife that would cut into my genitals. In the bathroom I gazed at my forlorn penis. At that moment I almost felt sorry for this poor thing dangling between my legs: I felt it was as innocent as I was in the whole affair. With these thoughts, I proceeded to shave my pubic area. The hair fell to the floor, leaving my penis in a state reminiscent of childhood. Clouds of steam inhibited my view; lost as I was in my reverie, I had forgotten to turn off the shower. Enveloped in this humid atmosphere, I felt as if I was lost in a dense fog. The time for the operation had come.

*

If you do not blench at the sight of blood and are not at all squeamish, it may interest you to follow me into the operating theatre. By now I am heavily sedated and unresponsive to what is going on around me. As the trolley trundles along the corridors to the theatre, lights dart past overhead; then the theatre doors are opened wide and I am manoeuvred on to the operating table. Moments later the anaesthetist inserts the butterfly needle into the back of my hand, and consciousness is lost. Nurses arrange my legs, so they are splayed high in the air. The surgeons are ready to begin.

If you have accompanied me this far, then you can observe the delicacy with which the surgeons perform their task. At their head, Mr Royle is handed a razor-sharp scalpel. The first incision is made, slitting the length of the penis from tip to base – revealing the glands that will be transformed into a clitoris. The crew mop their brows; instruments are passed from hand to hand; blood is staunched. Hidden within the penis, the outlet that will serve the purpose of a urethra is exposed. Lean forward and take a closer look, if you are having difficulty seeing. Projecting, it is snipped and re-routed, only to emerge lower down than before, though positioned above the neo-vagina. The pelvic floor muscles, stretched to their extremity, are prepared so they can be joined to the skin gathered from the penis. Another snip, and the scrotum is dismembered. Testicles, of no use, are ignominiously thrown aside, leaving a deflated-looking scrotal sack. Here Mr Royle finds material for constructing the labia. One final job and it will all be over: packing material is inserted to keep the vagina in place.

Surgery has been completed. Your visit to this work-shop that creates women is now over. You may follow me out, as I am wheeled into the recovery ward.

*

Everything was transfigured in to dim, blurred shapes surrounded by darkness. Vaguely, and with difficulty, I could make out the silhouettes of a television set and a wardrobe. Where was I? However hard I tried, I couldn't identify these surroundings. Brief moments of wakefulness repeatedly placed before my eyes the identical scene. Periods of oblivion alternated with these periods of disturbed consciousness – until I detected the distant voices of nurses, although I remained ignorant of the distinction between day and night. I was aware I was in hospital. The last memory I possessed was of being wheeled into the operating theatre. "It must all be over now," I thought. Then sleep encompassed me.

I did not wake again until the following morning. Through the gaps in the blinds bright, penetrating rays of sunshine danced across the bed. As I watched their movement I caught sight of the array of tubes sticking out of my body. Two protruded from my vagina, one a catheter, the other for blood drainage. Yet another ran from the back of my hand and was connected to a drip, the nature of which I was unaware of. A deep, relentless pain radiated from my genitals into the lower section of my abdomen. Unceasing, it was to be my constant companion for the next two months.

Amidst the discomfort, I found relief in the knowledge that all was for the best – that I had emerged from the operation a complete and whole woman. Gathering my concentration, I searched for the feeling I had anticipated encountering at this moment: the feeling of being a woman, without qualification. These musings were disturbed by the entrance of a nurse proffering pain killers. After the usual "How are you feeling?" and "Can I get anything for you?", she departed.

Breakfast was served at 9 o'clock – not a regular breakfast, though. I would not be enjoying a hearty "fry-up", no sausage, egg or bacon – not even a bowl of cereal or some fruit. For the next five days my diet was to be jelly for breakfast, jelly for lunch, and jelly for dinner. If I was lucky, I might have strawberry-flavour jelly in the morning and lime at lunch. All this jelly would be washed down with a cup of black tea, without sugar. The simple rationale behind this regime was the necessity of keeping me in a horizontal position. Any attempt towards the vertical would have resulted in disturbing the "pack", the apparatus that had been inserted into the vagina to keep it in place. It was thus imperative that defecation was avoided – for that could not, of course, be achieved lying down. During those first five days, jelly quickly became the bane of my existence.

On the sixth day after my operation, I was expecting the usual ration of jelly and black tea when Mr Royle entered my room – with a nurse close behind him, wheeling in some kind of respiratory equipment. The time had arrived for the removal of the "pack" in preparation for my return to the vertical. I knew what to expect; it had all been explained to me previously. But disturbing the centre of my pain was hardly an idea I relished. Nevertheless, realising the inevitability of the procedure, I resigned myself to fate and accepted the mask placed over my nose and mouth. The gas entered my lungs. My head became light, the surreal pervading the real. Lowering his glance to the site of surgery, Mr Royle slowly removed the pack from my vagina. After much twisting, easing and rotating, it suddenly slipped out, as if expelled from the rectum. The words "It's perfect – it looks fine!" impinged upon my drowsiness. A dilator was pushed into my vagina, and they both departed – Mr Royle having once again received the satisfaction of having created a woman.

Later that day, a nurse returned with a hand-held mirror and requested that I remove the dilator. Placing the mirror before my vagina, she gave me a guided tour of my new anatomy, carefully explaining the topography. "At the top, the most painful and sensitive area, is the clitoris; below it, the urethra, your new urinary outlet; and finally, at the very bottom, is the vaginal opening itself." All this was couched in headmistress-like tones with pronounced exactitude. Indeed, I was almost more intrigued by her style of articulation than the fact that my penis had been replaced with a vagina!

*

It is difficult to find some fresh and original way of describing the reaction I experienced towards my new genitalia. So much so that I am forced to echo the words of others and say that I felt this was exactly how things should be, and found it impossible to believe that I had ever possessed a penis. Yet perhaps this is not so different from the way one feels after experiencing any kind of surgery that dramatically and radically alters one's life.

Apart from returning to solid food once more – of which I took the greatest advantage – I spent the following days recovering my normal functions. On the 10th day I was discharged, and conveyed from Brighton to my flat in Kensington.

A New Beginning

The Sam/Samantha matrix had collapsed, leaving only Samantha in existence. The two tiers of my existence had become one. Thinking back to an earlier moment in my transition, I recalled that day when I had looked in the mirror hopefully searching for signs of Samantha. This time I knew I would look into the mirror with the certain knowledge that she had emerged in her entirety.

As I stood there looking at myself naked from head to toe, the completeness of my transition sent a shock surging through me. All the time, the being now in front of me had remained hidden inside Sam Hashimi, awaiting the moment of her birth. My face was soft, housing pretty feminine features and framed by a mane of blonde hair. Projecting from my tall, svelte frame, my breasts stood in proud and pert unison. And finally, below, there was the inverted triangle of hair that spoke of a woman's modesty. If even I could not believe that a man with a bristling moustache had once existed in place of this woman, how could anyone else conceive of such a thought?

For the first time, I experienced an overwhelming feeling of confidence in myself as a woman. Up to that moment I had felt disquieted by the secret knowledge I possessed about my genitalia. Not so any more! Henceforth I became the life and soul of every party, and danced my way through the clubs of London. My birth, my new beginning, demanded celebration of a kind I had never experienced before. From respectable clubs I received free membership, from their clientele invitations to dine in exclusive restaurants. And I was pursued by a constant stream of men, each more eager than the last to possess me.

To men, I seemed like a fascinating new toy. One by one they would approach me with the same lines, the same verbiage, I myself had once used as a man. In restaurants the waiters who once consigned to me the position of superiority now tacitly ignored me, only noting my existence by placing a napkin gently onto my lap. I missed the ritual of ordering in restaurants, and the conversations about football and the stock market. It was pointless for me to try to introduce these topics into conversation. The response would always be the same: "Your dress is very nice" or "You have beautiful eyes". In the end it all became rather tiresome – I felt as if I was being used, and I could see no way out of the cycle other than by avoiding relationships of this kind.

"Have I gone through all this in in order to remove one mask, only to replace it with another?", I pondered anxiously. Another characteristic of men that bothered me was their unremitting belief that women need to be protected. From where I was standing, it was precisely men who needed protecting from their tyrannical sex-drive! Often I longed to tell the men who entertained me that I myself had once been a man. Sometimes this desire even bordered on the irresistible. However, fear that their reaction might be aggressive, or simply the thought that they might abandon me, always deterred me from this course.

The relationships that I did succeed in developing were very short in duration, owing to my inability to tell men about my past. Very soon I discovered that I was more at ease in the company of women. Among the half-dozen women who comprise our little circle, I have found companionship and an enjoyable way to lead the life of a single girl.

*

Very soon I came to accept that however much one may alter the appearance of one's body – even to the extent of changing sex – the same mind, with the same problems, continues to persist within. My previous life will never be forgotten. My unhappy existence has turned me into a bitter, angry person: nothing seems to make me truly happy anymore.

My lost family will haunt me until the end of my days on earth. Often, even now, I wake up at night, because my sleep is tormented by nightmares about my lost children. During restless nights my childhood days in Baghdad, my parents and my siblings cry out to me for healing and resolution.

Throughout my life, from the days when I sneaked into my sister's room and replaced my clothes with hers, I have experienced feelings of guilt, as if I had indulged in some criminal act. The very circumstances in which I was constrained to enact these activities enveloped me in a appearance of wrongdoing. It was a matter of either casting aside my only source of comfort – and thus experiencing the torment of being excluded from the recognition of my female self – or continuing these activities and enduring the concomitant guilt. Either way, I could not win.

Being diagnosed as transsexual presented me with an opportunity to resolve the deceptions and subterfuge of my childhood. All that was needed was to reveal to my parents what I had been through during the past year. On numerous occasions after my visits to Dr Reid, I had telephoned my parents in Baghdad, determined to tell them that I was becoming a woman. But how could I broach such a revelation? "Hello mother, I don't know how to tell you this, but in December I'm having my penis replaced with a vagina!" I found it simply impossible to articulate such thoughts.

In the end, I decided I had to confront them in person, using my appearance to utter the words I could not express. I had given them some intimation that they should not expect to be meeting the same old Sam at the airport, but their reaction to this information was one of incomprehension. They would simply have to wait and see.

Because of the current political situation in Baghdad, my parents and I decided that we should meet in Amman, in Jordan. On landing, I hastily collected my luggage and proceeded to passport control. My parents were only a matter of minutes away from me now. Suitcases piled high upon a luggage trolley, I made my way to the arrival lounge. It had been almost 10 years since I last set eyes upon my parents, and I was no less curious than they were to descry the changes that time had inscribed upon their appearance.

Standing amidst a crowd of eager relations, agog with excited anticipation of the arrival of long-lost relatives, I recognised my mother and father – perhaps a little the worse for wear, yet in essence unmistakable, as all parents are. I waved and gestured to catch their attention as I moved closer towards them. Perhaps believing that I was just some particularly amiable individual, or that I had mistaken them for someone else, they smiled back politely, continuing to anticipate the arrival of their son. "It's me," I cried as I approached them, "Samantha. I used to be Sam!" My mother and father looked at one another in disbelief.

The import of what I had tried to tell them on the phone suddenly became completely clear. This was their daughter! Moments later, 10 years of absence terminatied in an onslaught of hugs and kisses.

Together we left the airport, firing a barrage of questions at one another, and made our way to our holiday apartment in Amman. The days that followed did not serve to quench their insatiable appetite for information about the course my life had taken over the last decade, and how I had ended up looking as I did. And though they had each accepted me as a woman at first sight, their address towards me constantly fluctuated between "he" and "she".

It was all very confusing! I will not say that they ever, during our stay in Jordan, became word-perfect in their ascription of my correct gender – but I can assert, without the least doubt, that both my mother and father came to accept me in my new role as their daughter, or rather their second daughter. In view of my regrettable exclusion from the knowledge that all Iraqi mothers pass on to their female offspring, my mother persisted on every possible occasion to redress this deficit by continuously trying to instill in me the decorum proper to a woman!

We had a delightful holiday together. And by the time I was due to return to London, my parents could hardly believe their daughter had once been their son.

Looking back upon the various occasions when I have travelled to Jordan, first as a man and later as a woman, the differences in the manner in which I was treated are abundantly clear. Being of Muslim orientation, Middle Eastern countries have the effect of making one especially aware of this distinction. Little needs to be said in relation to my experiences as a male: they are identical worldwide. As a woman, things are very different indeed.

I was born into a Muslim household. In my mother, as in other women around me, I perceived a being whose existence was rigidly circumscribed. In almost every aspect of their lives, they appeared to experience the strictest constraints. I saw women forced into careers that held no interest for them, into marriages contracted and enforced by unyielding parents. It seemed to be the woman who represented the catalyst of sin; the scheming temptress, who at all costs had to be hidden from man. And the woman who instigated the crimes of rape and adultery, not a man with lascivious designs. In the eyes of orthodox Muslims, a transsexual woman was a sin against God.

But what was the origin of such contorted and unjust notions? Perhaps it was part of the Prophet's design to emancipate woman in the fullness of time, with the dawning of a new social order? Maybe history had taught him that any equalisation of society invariably resulted in disorder. Bearing in mind the consequences of the liberation of slaves and the equality with their masters that it bestowed upon them, it may have seemed inopportune to countenance the equality of women. But that was 1500 years ago. Why were the shackles still in place today?

*

As a class, it is usual for women to be treated with a certain degree of respect and politeness that is absent from social attitudes towards men. Whether for better or worse, women are regarded as generally more vulnerable than men, more helpless in the face of threats and abuse. With this and similar thoughts in mind, I arrived back in London, intent on attempting to resolve the difficulties that existed between myself and the mother of my children. I believed that my change of sex might have the effect of assuaging the past.

Realising that the only chance of renewing contact with my children lay in establishing a friendly relationship with their mother, I finally decided to contact my first ex-wife. But, although she had known me for no less than 13 years and was the mother of our children, she simply could not take on board the changes that I had undergone. In response to my initial "Hello", she stood awkwardly in the doorway, not knowing how to receive this stranger and vigorously searching her memory. I waited patiently, adopting a similar expression to hers. An interval of about a minute passed, at the conclusion of which a noticeable change came over her expression – one that was not hostile, but seemed more of a conscious attempt to determine precisely how she was going to receive me. She was utterly nonplussed and simply did not know what to do with herself. Reaching for a jacket, she stepped from her doorway. "Let's go for a walk" were her only words.

Fastening the buttons on her little pink Chanel jacket to keep out the cold, she led the way as we walked along the tree-lined avenues, exchanging a few superficial words with one another. Just as she had failed to identify me as I stood on her doorstep, so too did I find it difficult to associate her with the woman who had been my wife. Beside me walked an acquaintance of yester-year – a different girl, who I had chanced to meet while walking in the fresh spring air. Nevertheless, I cannot say that the feelings of love I once felt for her had completely dissipated.

At what I believed to be an appropriate moment, I introduced the subject that had led me to contact her. Without artifice, I begged her to forget the past and to seek in the future a peaceful and lasting friendship. "How I've missed the children," I began. "I haven't seen them or heard from them for two years now – I don't even know what they look like anymore!" She hesitated, knowing that my reappearance heralded nothing but trouble and searching for words that would discourage me from attempting to stay in touch. "My boyfriend wouldn't like it" was her eventual response. But, perhaps through pity, together with the desire to end the contention between us, she offered to try to re-establish contact for me with our children. When our walk ended, we parted on what seemed to be amicable terms.

The new optimism of the previous day dragged me prematurely from my night's sleep. Anxiously, I awaited the coming day. Was it only the birds and myself who were awake at this time of morning? At 9 o'clock I would contact my ex-wife's solicitor and discuss with him the matter of the children. But my enthusiasm was very quickly dispelled. Without prior warning, a complaint of harassment had been filed with the police. Impeded by a blockade of lawyers and policemen, I had to adopt other methods of contacting my children.

*

Eagerly I scribbled one letter after another – as if I would thereby be reunited with my children all the quicker. Page upon page I filled with pleas for mercy, offering a candid appeal to love, as only the hopeless can. Images of my daughter's sweet face convinced me that from such a one nothing but sympathy could issue. Her birthday was approaching – she would be 13 this year. "Please let this be the last year that I am denied the right to hold her close, whispering 'Happy birthday' delicately in her ear." With these thoughts, I sealed the envelope and enclosed it with her birthday present, along with letters to other members of the family.

My forebodings proved only too well founded. Silence was the unmitigated reply. Once again I contacted my ex-wife's solicitor. "I'm terribly sorry," ran his excuse, "but the fact of your sex change might be disturbing for the children." Whatever would come next? For perhaps the first time, I began to realise that I would probably never see my children again. My entire life had been a history of self-deception! Why should the law favour me against such outstanding odds? My only comfort was tears.

The ambiguous identity of Sam Hashimi and Samantha Kane notwithstanding, was I not owed some measure of mercy – if for no other reason, then on humanitarian grounds? Was it unreasonable to want to possess a recent photograph, a school report, a letter from one's children? The inhumanity of my position was only compounded further by the very element that should have offered me a source of justification for the actions of the past: *transsexualism.* One would have to go very far to find a disorder that evokes so great a degree of prejudice, that is so immune to the pleas of reason.

Shortly after my second discussion with the lawyer, I obtained a letter from a consultant psychiatrist stating that my change of sex could in no way have a detrimental effect on my children. In fact, it would be beneficial for them to know me as I am now.

However, I fear I must reconcile myself to the futility of my quest and bear the anguish of my lost paternity without complaint. The only cries of pain or protest that I seem able to utter without bringing trouble upon myself are those that accompany tears. Now that loss of hope has attached itself to my endeavours, perhaps it should not come as a surprise that I seldom enjoy a night's undisturbed repose? Or that my happiness is always quashed before it even begins to develop?

So long as I am exiled from my children, my life will always be lived under the shadow of that knowledge. Nevertheless, I continue to press forward from day to day, as if the future holds the key to my problems.

With my mother in Jordan.

My father accepted me as his daughter.

Having fun by the Dead Sea.

Back in Business

Six months have now elapsed since my operation. Not surprisingly, after such an extended period of disruption, I find myself once again confronted with the mundane necessity of earning a living. At 38 years of age, it is also necessary to provide for the future. "What would Sam Hashimi have done in my position?", I asked myself. He would have taken the problem by the throat, and thrown his weight around! Somehow I feel that the time is over for such aggressive tactics; that I must utilise my new attributes as a pretty and feminine woman. At least, I shall not ignore this new prerogative. Whatever else may have altered, my business acumen remains the same, notwithstanding the change of exterior.

One is always aware of a tendency as a transsexual to hyperfeminise oneself – to adopt the artificial stereotypes attributed to women, in order to convince oneself and others that one is indeed a woman. Such tendencies attach themselves to insecurity, and I myself was once a practitioner of this type of affectation. In adopting a soft and vulnerable appearance, it had been my primary aim. Later I realised that my position as a woman would in no way be jeopardised if I acted naturally. What was the use of playing the helpless female in the cut-and-thrust of the business world? The suggestion was ludicrous. In place of the hyper-feminised Samantha, there emerged a modern woman in the true sense of the word – one, sharp and flexible, and able to make decisions.

Dusting the cobwebs off Sam's business brain, I set myself the task of developing my skills in new training and research, finally launching a media and publishing company. It was all-out war. Directing my assault at certain sectors of the market, I went in with all guns blazing. There was nothing for it, I reasoned, but to fight to the death for the life that had been stolen from me; to build an empire of proportions that would overshadow everything I had attempted in the past!

World Cup '98 was my first project. An untiring taskmaster, I laboured day and night to make sure that my new magazine would be launched on time. The most skilled graphic designers wearied under my continuous demands to improve on designs that they had reworked a hundred times already. I sought interviews with untiring determination, among the players in France. Articles, photographs, interviews – everything had to be ready, or the entire project would fall to the ground. It was the most difficult thing – to be taken seriously as a woman in so masculine a world as that of football.

Finally, everything was ready and waiting to go to the printers. But then an unexpected problem occurred: our computer crashed and everything – all the work that had been prepared over the previous weeks – was gone! It was exasperating! Immediately, we withdrew the magazine and prepared to cover the later stages of the World Cup. At the time of writing, I am waiting for the Football Association to provide me with clearance so I can gain access to the players in France. Meanwhile, myself and a friend are working without respite to get this book to the printers on time.

So far as the immediate present is concerned, with the launch of this book, I have to face the press and exchange the position of interviewer for that of interviewee. Then I shall forge ahead, as a journalist myself, gathering information around the clock for a variety of magazines – finance, women's issues, property and entertainment.

Ultimately, however, I must live my life the same way as any other woman. But simply to live thus is a boon to me after so many years of turmoil and unhappiness – to live in peace and to live as the person I am.